6

HABITS

of

Highly
Effective
Teams

6

HABITS

of

Highly
Effective
Teams

Stephen E. Kohn and Vincent D. O'Connell

CAREER
PRESS
Franklin Lakes, NJ

6 HABITS OF HIGHLY EFFECTIVE TEAMS
EDITED AND TYPESET BY KARA REYNOLDS
Cover design by Jeffrey Bailey/Solaris Design Group
Printed in the U.S.A. by Book-mart Press

To order this title, please call toll-free 1-800-CAREER-1 (NJ and Canada: 201-848-0310) to order using VISA or MasterCard, or for further information on books from Career Press.

CAREER
PRESS

The Career Press, Inc., 3 Tice Road, PO Box 687,
Franklin Lakes, NJ 07417
www.careerpress.com

Library of Congress Cataloging-in-Publication Data

Kohn, Stephen E., 1957-
    6 Habits of highly effective teams / by Stephen E. Kohn and Vincent D. O'Connell.
        p. cm.
    Includes index.
    ISBN-13: 978-156414-927-5
    ISBN-10: 1-56414927-7
    1. Teams in the workplace—Management. I. O'Connell, Vincent D., 1959- II. Title. III. Title: Six habits of highly effective teams.

HD66 K64 2007
658.4′022--dc22

2007007244

Dedication

For all our past, current, and future teammates.

6

Acknowledgments

I would like to thank an important teammate of mine, my brother Mike, who reviewed segments of this manuscript in advance, and provided useful thoughts and encouragement. Mike's long and successful career in branch management for financial services organizations has engendered significant expertise in facilitating teamwork directed toward meeting goals of the corporate enterprise. His viewpoints and feedback were extremely useful from this perspective of real-life team leadership within a highly competitive industry. But as importantly, he and I shared so many athletic team experiences when we were younger, and they all helped frame the attributes of excellent teamwork that Steve Kohn and I tried to convey in this book. It was fun to reminisce about teams we played on, and their respective characteristics. So, thanks for your help, brother.

Vincent D. O'Connell
Fairfax Station, Va.

Contents

FIGURES

Foreword

The benefits of effective teamwork are apparent for any organization that forms teams to conduct its business. In simplest terms, teams are built to add value for the client or other direct beneficiaries of the team's work. The premise is that a collection of people with complementary skills will produce better results, getting the project done more efficiently and more effectively than a process involving independently delegated tasks with little coordinated effort.

One of the roles I perform as a manager involves helping my organization establish teams and evaluate their output. On the surface, it may seem to be a rather mechanical process to populate a team with the right people. What needs to occur, one might think, is simply to identify:

▶ The skill sets that the team needs.

▶ The people who own these skill sets.

▶ The respective time availability of these identified people to become engaged in a new team project.

When the available and qualified pool has been uncovered, there might be a "down-select" from that point using a "best athlete" approach, until all the team's slots are filled. But for those of us whose job it is to build very important teams with the right combination of talent, other considerations enter into the equation:

▶ Does this team, as constituted, possess people whose perspectives are broad enough to understand and integrate the "bigger picture" organizational and client issues that will need to be considered?

▶ How much overall project team experience does this team possess? How much of this experience is on projects of a similar size, scope, and complexity compared to the one for which this team is being built?

▶ Is the team leader's project management style a good fit with this team?

▶ How much coaching and mentoring is this team likely to need from external sources?

And perhaps most importantly:

▶ Is this group likely to work well together?

Teams that my organization assembles need to have the capability to comprehend bigger picture issues that impact on their decision-making. For a large enterprise such as the one where I work, there are vast, interconnected networks of internal and external stakeholders that are likely to pertain to the functions of any team we put together. Consequently, a sense of the bigger picture is crucial to understanding that there are often broader implications that affect team planning activities. A prudent team-building strategy for any size organization will focus on more than ensuring that sufficient knowledge or experience exists within the team—it will focus on ensuring that the team demonstrates a willingness and aptitude to explore all the factors that contribute to achieving the organization's comprehensive goals. Team members may possess relevant expertise congruent with the team's stated purpose, but if their approach to their team tasks is narrow and myopic, the value of the team's eventual output may suffer.

The overriding principle, then, is that team effectiveness is a function not just of the expertise that team members possess, but also of the behaviors that define an approach to accomplishing the team's overall goals. It is a perspective on team-building and teamwork that similarly takes into account a bigger picture. The broader perspective is that behavioral considerations are what drive the value inherent in any shared team effort.

This is the broad theme of *6 Habits of Highly Effective Teams*, and it is why I find the book so very useful. Teams need to incorporate proven behavioral habits that facilitate the building of a cohesive unit. This book grounds us in what these superior team habits are, and provides excellent case examples, thought-provoking questions, and team evaluation tools to reinforce the book's valuable insights.

I believe that effective teams do possess the habits advocated in this book. Further, I believe that these habits are, in essence, an extension of the sponsoring organization's "corporate culture," which reflects values and norms shared by people and groups, and guides the way people need to interact with each other to foster a superior, productive work environment. One of the reasons I connected so strongly with the contents of this book is that the habits largely mirror my organization's corporate culture and its behavioral expectations. When team habits are aligned with corporate culture, all aspects of work performance—inside and outside of teams—are guided by the same value set, and thereby the entire organizational system works together more fluently and synergistically.

In that spirit, the six habits of highly effective teams are really part of the best habits of effective organizations, and of the people who work within them.

I extend to you my personal best wishes in your efforts to incorporate these habits into your organization, its teams, and your personal skill set.

Dr. Lyla El-Sayed
R&D Manager
E.I. Dupont, Parlin, N.J.

Preface

As coauthors of three books now, we have established ourselves as a team. It's a small team—as small a team as can be assembled, we suppose, because it has only two members. But our work together has always been a team effort. We have understood our respective roles, and we have worked collaboratively toward the objective of completing these writing projects. For this particular book, identifying ourselves as a team helped us a great deal, as we needed to connect to the concepts of effective teamwork. We met often in the earliest stages of the project, to consider the themes we hoped to convey and the information we needed to gather. In the forefront of these discussions were the needs of our eventual customer—you, the reader, who wish to advance your knowledge and skills in team leadership and team participation. We wanted to be as creative as possible, and our team interactions to generate new ideas utilized the methods we discuss in this book. Eventually, we made our way to our computers, and began implementing our project plan. Throughout this effort, we encountered, and then needed to work through, many of the same emotional issues and nuances that far larger teams face, on a much smaller scale. We focused on remaining a cohesive unit by communicating often, working through any differences we had, and making the substantive decisions that needed to be made about ways to share our team-building model.

But this tiny team we formed is just one of many in which we have participated in our respective lives and careers. In preparing our ideas, we recalled so many of our respective group experiences: a highly successful high school baseball team coached by a man who is now the head coach of a world champion professional basketball franchise, and a closely knit account management team that sold more new business than any of its peer groups throughout the country. We also considered the dysfunctional teams we have observed while performing our training programs and consulting practice within organizations—a few of which, we openly admit, we were a part of ourselves. The great teams stuck in our mind, and the bad ones left strong impressions too. As has most everyone, we have learned from positive team models, as well as from the pain of team dysfunction or failure. The more teams one joins, the more likely one is to have both positive and not-so-great shared group experiences. But that is why we wanted to write this book—to increase the odds of your team experience being effective, mutually productive, stimulating, and enjoyable.

To all of our past teammates—in athletics, academics, and in our combined professional careers—we say thank you for your implicit contribution to this book. In addition, both of us are part of families, and we want to acknowledge them for guiding our thinking. The values we share and the emotional resonance we have with our family "team" is a constant form of inspiration for us, in all aspects of our personal and professional lives.

Stephen E. Kohn
Vincent D. O'Connell

PART I

Introduction

Imagine you have just been offered a job, and as the hiring manager approaches you, she smiles, and exclaims to you heartily, "Welcome to the team!"

It's a statement that conveys more than just the recognition that you are about to become part of the group that's hired you. It's a statement that engenders warmth and good feelings, because the word *team* conveys something special—a sense that you are both wanted and *accepted*. Teams are more than simply groups. One might say that *team* is to *group* as *comrade* or *buddy* is to *friend*. The respective terms may be used rather interchangeably, but make no mistake—there is a slight but distinct difference in connotation between these pairs of words. The connotation of *team* is one to which we connect in a very positive and emotionally resonant way.

It is what makes team formation, team-building, and team performance such fascinating phenomena. It is why the two of us love to work on building, coaching, and training teams. There is complexity to teams, combining the hard realities of organizational performance expectations with the integral human relations elements that are as diverse and difficult to decipher as people themselves. Teams are intriguing to observe and analyze, and our work with them offers an unending range of personal and professional gratification.

Much of what we will be describing throughout this book considers the emotional aspects of effective teamwork. So we would like to use this introduction to "tee up" some of our thinking about the psychology of teams, to prepare you for the principles we will emphasize and the behavioral recommendations we will make. These are rather random reflections on teams and teamwork, but they tie closely to the content we include in the remainder of the book. We hope that by sharing some philosophies and perspectives on the immensely interesting concept of teamwork, here in this preliminary introduction, we will whet your appetite a bit about this topic before we get into the nitty-gritty of explaining our practical team-building guidelines.

Our formative experiences with teams

Like many people, our initial experience with the psychology of teams occurred rather early in our lives, through participation in and observation of various athletic team endeavors. During the school day, we attended and participated in prearranged groups called "classes": English class, math class, science class, and so on. But once the school day was over, we were no longer part of a class, but part of a team. The sports we played after school changed from season to season, but the value of being on a team was a consistent part of our early lives. The teams to which we belonged represented more than the school we attended or the community where we lived; they represented for us a sense of who we were. We recall instances when we and many of our schoolmates would frame our very identity based on the team to which we belonged. As part of a football team, our hair was cut very short, and we needed to manifest an aggressive, slightly nasty edge to our interpersonal attitude at times. For hockey, the team was about fun, roughhousing, and the slightly insane shared team sacrifice of having to attend practices at ungodly hours—before dawn or late into the night—usually in the bitter cold. The point is that each team in which we participated bonded a bit differently, and morphed our personalities a bit differently as well.

It was, in many ways, the best time of our lives.

Speaking of teeing up...

Actually, some sports or group endeavors are more team-oriented than others. There are sports such as swimming or track and field that form *around* teams, but the sport itself is a highly individual effort. In these sports, participants root for teammates, but the competition itself is essentially an individual pursuit of one's personal best. But it is fascinating to observe what happens when athletes in these types of individual sports get thrown into a more traditional team experience. For some, it is as if an innate, pent-up psychological need to be a true teammate is finally met. A classic case of this has been occurring around the biennial Ryder Cup golf competition between the European continent's team and the best golfers from the United States. The sport of golf is highly individualistic, but for this one event, team concepts do apply. Members can help each other read putts, communicate about strategy, make decisions about whether to concede a putt to the opposition, and apply other team aspects of the competition. For some reason, the European team seems to embrace the team concept far better than the U.S. team. The European golfers show incredible team cohesion, a strong sense of togetherness, and their performance reflects their psychological immersion in the team experience—it has been simply outstanding. During the past few competitions, which were deemed rather even on paper, the Europeans have absolutely trounced the American team. For reasons that seem tied to the respective teams' interpersonal dynamics, the European team over-performs and U.S. team underperforms. Most observers—including the players themselves—attribute this uneven competition not to respective talent, but to the fact that the European players have somehow bonded better, and have applied team principles to the competition, thereby gaining the competitive edge.

Sports-to-business analogies are sometimes risky to make, but this one in particular seems relevant. We may pursue our career along a very personal track, focused on increasing our individual skills and competencies, but there is something special about participating on a team. The simple fact is that for most of us, nothing feels better than a team victory!

The psychological complexity of teams

Indeed, there are complex forces at work in teams, which greatly affect performance. There are three aspects of team psychology that stand out to us: *affinity*, *belonging*, and *altruism*.

The psychology of teams implies the need to address humans' social needs, which have deeply psychodynamic, as well as environmental, roots. The psychodynamic issues at play in teams are tied to unconscious factors driving affinity-based social behaviors, individuation and separation issues within our families, and a general propensity to share and help out others in a larger community. Teamwork connects us to our innate drive to belong and to demonstrate altruism. We affiliate with those who share our values, and when we do, we wish to help out, and share of ourselves. It gets us outside the loneliness of solo efforts and gets us connected to others who have common purposes, objectives, and beliefs.

The opposite of altruism is narcissism. More narcissistic personality types have difficulty in groups because their tendencies are to frame everything that happens and everything that should happen around themselves. In Greek mythology, Narcissus was a handsome and conceited young man who spurned the advances of many, including the nymph Echo and the young man Ameinias, to whom Narcissus gave a sword, telling Ameinias to prove his love. Ameinias, hurt in his pride, killed himself with the sword and cursed Narcissus, wishing that he would never possess the object of his love. One day, Narcissus bowed to drink from a water fountain. Seeing his own face reflected on the water, he fell in love with it. Narcissus was so attracted to his own image that he frequently returned to the water fountain to contemplate himself. Thus he went on languishing until his death. Another version of the legend is that, seeing himself on the water, he tried to embrace his own image and drowned in the attempt. At that drowning site, according to the legend, a new flower sprouted that takes the name of its unhappy creator—the narcissus.

Sigmund Freud added the term *narcissism* to the vocabulary of psychology to designate love of the self-image, and the stage of development when a child makes his or her own self the main object of his or her love. These ideas have given rise to many studies that describe and analyze the distinct profile of the developmentally stunted narcissistic personality. According to the Diagnostic and Statistical Manual of Mental Disorders (*DSM IV*) of the American Psychiatric Association, narcissists are arrogant and conceited individuals who have magnificent fantasies about themselves. They overestimate their success, need to be constantly admired, and always expect preferential treatment. Narcissists are convinced that they deserve more than they receive. They are worried about looking good and keeping themselves young. They are insensitive to the needs and problems of other people. With little tolerance for criticism, they often react with fury to real or imaginary slights. They have never grown out of the stage when they believed the world revolved around them!

Interestingly, from an epidemiological perspective, narcissists tend more often to be males rather than females.

The purpose of this book is not to facilitate a clinical, psychodiagnostic approach to work within teams at the workplace. We don't want you out there in teams labeling each other as narcissists! That is neither practical nor useful in any way. But here is a little early, advance piece of advice for you, about the makeup of teams and how to ensure that teams maintain the potential to be highly effective:

Narcissists just do not make very good teammates!

If that makes sense to you now, you are well-positioned to absorb the rest of this book.

People styles

In *6 Habits of Highly Effective Bosses*, we explained how the human race seemed to be rather equally divided among four "people styles":

1. The highly assertive, highly responsive Expressives.
2. The highly assertive but less responsive Drivers.
3. The highly responsive but less assertive Amiables.
4. The less assertive, less responsive Analyticals.

What tendencies do these personality types bring to teams? We believe that even in their purest form (which is rather rare, as people tend to have a dominant style but blend in other styles at times), these people styles all work well in teams, provided the role to which they are assigned is largely synchronous with their people style. For example, a team's sales-oriented duties are the strength of **Expressives**. Task leadership roles are consistent with the **Drivers'** people style. Team support-oriented duties are effectively carried out by **Amiables**. And of course, **Analyticals** are great in financial or budgeting roles. If you need a review of these styles, read *People Styles at Work*, written by Robert and Dorothy Bolton, or look through the overview we present in our previous book. These psychological insights about matching people to roles and "flexing" to people with different styles to build rapport can be extremely helpful to teams.

Teams are sponsored, and compete

In our early brainstorming about the general concepts underlying the term *team*, one of us noted to the other that our respective alma maters have clubs that play rugby. They are not specifically labeled officially as teams—a designation that distinguishes this sport from others due to the fact that it falls outside the auspices of universities' formal athletic programs. And it raises an interesting point: Teams (more than "groups" or "clubs") tend to be sponsored by some organized entity.

The Rugby Club was designated a club by the university because it was not a sponsored, subsidized sport, but the players deemed it a team. In large part, this label was due to the fact that rugby players compete. When groups compete, they are likely to be referred to as a team.

People with shared interests, for example, tend to form a "club" or a "community network." However, people who engage in any type of competition against another group tend to call themselves a "team." High school kids with common interests form clubs, such as the Political Science Club or the Shakespeare Club. But if a school group is formed to compete against another school by answering questions accurately and more quickly about political science or Shakespeare (or other questions applicable to the fund of knowledge high school students should have), the group they form will most likely be labeled a team. Teams compete.

Perhaps this is why organizations are attracted to doing business in teams. There is an action-orientation to the team concept, a competitive aspect inherent in teams and teamwork. Businesses know they are always in competition, for customers and customer loyalty, for new business, and for method improvement that will make them more efficient than others in the same business. The concept of teams is consistent with an organization's imperative to push forward knowing that there are others in the industry doing the same. Whether it is this type of implied competition or more direct, head-to-head competition, organizational teams form when someone is keeping score or making qualitative judgments about one business versus another. And when there is indeed a bona fide competition for new clients occurring, led by account management or business development marketing teams, the group almost certainly will be labeled a team. Nowadays, in a business context, any group organized for the purpose of direct competitive activities against another group really *needs* to be labeled a "team."

Teams aggregate expertise

However, the team concept is not all about forming an entity that can engage in competition. Teams also *aggregate expertise* into one, single, collective effort. Teams form so there is a structure into which expertise can be placed to meet a need of the enterprise (usually, a customer-focused need). The team concept is largely about this sense of shared expertise and having a structural means by which this expertise can be transformed into value. When we join an organizational team, we should be bringing more expertise to the group than it had without our participation. If this expertise is irrelevant or beyond the scope of the team's mission, then our expertise is best leveraged outside the structure of the team—that is, it should be deemed an external resource to the team, not a member of the team itself. It is a subtle distinction to make, but the point is that teams have focus, and the team entity's purpose is to put together the specific expertise needed to achieve success. *accomplish something*

Teamwork is fun

Ask the European Ryder Cup team, and they will tell you that they never enjoyed themselves practicing their profession as much as when they won as a team. Individual accomplishment is personally rewarding, for sure. But teamwork is fun! It taps into gratifications that simply cannot be attained in solo efforts. So our focus in this book is more than simply on helping people optimize their team's productivity. It is directed toward people enjoying their work, and balancing the hard, economic realities of meeting job performance expectations with the opportunity to achieve both pleasure and gratification from the pursuit of personal, economic, and occupational goals.

CHAPTER 1

Resonating With a Team Experience

I felt like I belonged with these men. We read one another's feelings and moods and adapted accordingly. We were Connected. Our structure and leadership emerged from the circumstances of the moment. We valued and respected each other. Our relationships felt right. When we had conflicts, we worked them out ourselves....We trusted each other. We gave our time and talents to one another and utilized our skills and knowledge effectively. We worked hard and we had fun. —Tom Heuerman, Ph.D.

What was the best team in which you ever participated? If an answer comes quickly and vividly to mind, then this team experience must resonate with you still, in a special sort of way. Something magical happened—a confluence of favorable behaviors and circumstances came together, at a special time in a special place with a special group of people, all working together on a special project for a special internal or external client. The results and the team experience itself were amazing—no doubt, they exceeded even the high expectations you and your teammates had when the team was first formed.

What exactly happened on a day-to-day basis within this "best team" experience, from the outset on forward? What were this team's characteristics? How was it led? How did team members communicate and relate with each other? How did it handle difficulties, disagreements, and conflicts, and remain focused on the project's objectives rather than allowing the problems to delay or undermine the team's efforts? And perhaps most of all, what were the intrinsic factors, such as group norms and interpersonal expectations by team members, that caused this experience to engender such a long-standing positive feeling from you about the team experience?

In the workshops, training classes, and team coaching projects that our firm conducts, we like to raise this "best team" question to get our customers focused on models of team excellence. We have heard hundreds and hundreds of individuals describe literally thousands of memorable team project experiences within all types of organizations and industries. From this data, and supported by other team effectiveness research done in the workplace, we have concluded that superior team attributes tend to cluster around several significant "habits"—behaviors and attitudes—that add the most value to the process of working as a team. Effective teams are driven far less by the individual technical competencies of their members, we have learned, and far more by a group of six transcendent human relations and group process factors.

In fact, several of these factors mirror the human relations behaviors and attitudes we described in *6 Habits of Highly Effective Bosses*. That book focused on skills for **organizational leadership and individual development**. It emphasized building people skills for motivating subordinates and supervising their performance. Leadership is a relationship, we espoused, between an individual who does the leading and a different individual or a group of followers being led. Teams, alternatively, are often formed to implement and coordinate projects. In our present consideration of the habits of highly effective teams, we are less interested in skills that foster organizational leadership and individual development, and far more attentive to skills that facilitate **project success and group development**. Individual human relations skills power leadership. Group human relations skills power teamwork.

Although only one of the habits we describe includes the word *relationship* in it, all six habits are, in essence, relationship-focused. In many ways, a focus on relationship skills as the core component of effective teams is self-evident; certainly, it is far easier to grasp than a consideration of the same concept in the context of 1:1 supervision. For example, autocratic, command-and-control type managers might see effectiveness in their organizational leadership role involving a wide range of planning and resource allocation skills that have little to do with the quality of their relationships with direct reports. In comparison, the concepts of superior relationship skills and team excellence are integrally intertwined. The fact that relationship skills drive teamwork is borne out of the dynamics of individuals joining together for the purpose of getting something accomplished. Teams are groups, and the very definition of a team or group involves cooperative efforts driven by how well people relate to each other. Consequently, this book needs to be less concerned with making the case that relationship skills matter to teams, and more concerned with *which of these skills matter most, and the best way to learn and incorporate them, so they can manifest themselves in a resonant team experience.*

In essence, although many of the human relations habits of effective teams are the same as those characteristic of a single individual exercising supervisory leadership, there are significant differences in how the skills are developed and applied in teams. The team paradigm creates a far different context within which these skills are performed than that of individual leadership. Team skill-building considers a distinct and unique set of group priorities, challenges, and interpersonal phenomena. Exercises to build teamwork skills are inevitably oriented toward creating the kind of resonance inside the team that occurred in your personal "best team" model. As Daniel Goleman, the best-selling author and prominent organizational consultant pointed out in a 2002 interview with Leader to Leader:

> On a team, resonance releases energy in people, and it increases the amount of energy available to the team, which, in turn, puts people in a state where they can work at their best. The dictionary defines resonance as the propagation of sound "by synchronous vibration." On a resonant team, the members vibrate together, so to speak, with positive emotional energy.

That is, in essence, the objective of our 6 Habits model of team effectiveness—to help members tune in to each other, to synchronize, to share energy, and thereby, to perform at their best within a resonant group experience.

Both team membership and team leadership roles are applicable to our discussion of the factors that make a team effective. Team membership skills require acceptance that an entity exists to which to relate—the team. Team leadership requires a parallel paradigm shift, from a focus on gaining an understanding of supervised individuals, to gaining an understanding of the group itself within which individuals operate in a coordinated way. Effectiveness in each role—as a team member and as a team leader—requires an appreciation of the dynamics of group behavior and the premise that the team "whole" can be understood at least as well as the individual parts that form it.

CHAPTER 2

Defining Teams and Team Effectiveness

Team: A group of interacting individuals sharing a common goal and the responsibility for achieving it. —The Quality Assurance Project's definition of *team*

What makes groups of people excel and add value by working together in the pursuit of organizational objectives, far more than soloist efforts that have no real interest in group relationships? Certainly, team success is contingent upon many factors. The starting point in describing the factors behind team excellence must be an effort to establish a fundamental understanding of what the term *team* means. Then we can gain a better understanding of the concept of team effectiveness.

The fact is that the label *team* is used so widely and so often that it is hard to pinpoint exactly what the term means anymore. It can be used as broadly as simply being synonymous with any group of people with some shared purpose. For example, it is not unusual for the biggest organizations in the world to label themselves as a team to try and foster a sense of team identity within the respective company. But this macro-level label of a team is quite different than the context of the project team within these same organizations, formed to address a very specific company need or client requirement.

Team definitions vary. After Susan Cohen and Diane Bailey, a pair of management researchers, conducted an extensive review of team effectiveness literature for the *Journal of Management*, the definition of a team that they established was as follows:

> A team is a collection of individuals who are interdependent in their tasks, who share responsibility for outcomes, who see themselves and are seen by others as an intact social entity embedded in one or more larger social systems (for example, business unit or the corporation), and who manage their relationships across organizational boundaries.

In a very successful book on the subject, called *The Wisdom of Teams*, J.R. Katzenbach and D.K. Smith define a team in a similar way. They describe a team as:

...a small number of people with complementary skills who are committed to a common purpose, performance goals, and approach for which they hold themselves mutually accountable.

We believe that we need to ground our model in an understanding of the types of groups to which our 6 Habits model applies best, so that members of real teams can identify with and leverage the factors that we discuss. Using Katzenback and Smith's useful team definition, our concept of highly effective teams refers to excellence by groups with *highly complementary skills* who are committed to *highly common objectives* and *highly common performance goals*, for which they hold themselves *highly accountable*. By adding a high-to-low gradient to the defining features of a team, and by focusing only on a narrow set of groups in which much higher levels of interdependency apply, we believe we are adding more practical applications to the skill development we advocate. The exact maximum number of members on a team—the "small number of people" that Katzenback and Smith refer to in their definition—is not one that we wish to set in stone. However, this "small number" must be circumscribed enough so that the dynamics of group interdependence are quite real and palpable. The fact is, when the team to which one belongs broadens in size, the human relations dynamics of team interdependence, mission, performance goals, and mutual accountability tend to become more diffuse—and as such, less meaningful. While there might not be a magical number to the specific size of the team to which the skills we discuss in this book apply most, we will posit, for contextual purposes, that the statistical mode (the number that occurs most frequently in a set of values—not the average or the range) for the number of team members for which our model applies best is somewhere between six and 30. The range is large because groups of different sizes can be labeled appropriately as a team in a certain set of circumstances, and our model is quite relevant to all of them. The factors that matter most are these high levels of complementary skills, common objectives, common performance goals, and mutual accountability. The smallness of the number of people on a team is conveyed best by the degree to which these defining features within the team truly apply.

Additionally, the group must be highly interdependent and see themselves as an "intact social entity." They must meet often, or interact extensively through more virtual communication methods, to establish this interdependence and identity as a distinct unit. The types of team issues we discuss are not nearly as applicable for a group that calls itself a team, for whatever reason, but only meets or interacts on a very intermittent or irregular basis.

As such, the team model from which we work is more geared to the *project* than it is to other types of teams. A project team implies a group performing a circumscribed set of activities over a preestablished time frame, following a schedule and plan with milestones that help gauge progress toward the common objectives. A project context brings high relevance to team effectiveness skills as we describe them in this book.

A project team tends to have:

▶ **A small number of people.** Project teams are assigned based on the project's scope and requirements. Ideally, team assignments are made with organizational efficiencies in mind. The organization does not wish either to overpopulate or underpopulate a team to complete a particular project's scope of work. To overpopulate the project team is wasteful of time and resources, and to underpopulate it is to risk project delays due to resource shortages. Therefore, the smallest number of people possible necessary to get the work done well should be on a team. When the project scope broadens, and the team grows, the "small number of people" criterion for describing an applicable team may be nullified. In this case, a narrower, mini-project team within the same overall program may be the best model.

▸ **Complementary skills.** Ideally, project teams bring together the right mix of different people owning relevant skills and understandings. Members' skills, qualifications, and competencies are a key component of a team member's selection for project participation in the first place. Projects are good models for the team concept because they require a selection process that matches the scope of work requirements with the people who have the skills to apply to that work. Additionally, these respective skills necessary to meet scope of work requirements should complement each other, or be applied in a way that adds value by bringing the requisite skills together for a particular purpose. Complementary skills accelerate the team's performance, because work can be done concomitantly. Synergies become possible when members' respective competencies mesh together well. The right combination of skills can create a catalytic, "2 + 2 = 8" effect that offers opportunities for exponentially higher levels of performance. A project team is an ideal group for planning ways to blend competencies—sometimes even using members' skills through subcontractual arrangements—to meet and exceed the scope of the work requirements.

▸ **A common purpose.** For a group of individuals to be transformed into a team, they must have a purpose that is distinctive, specific to the group, and promotes member buy-in to a whole that becomes greater than simply collecting individual contributions toward the same objective. Project teams are good models for the team concept because projects tend to have a preidentified purpose that members can easily understand and work toward. Projects tend to commence based on articulated mission statements and evident purposes. A project framework is ideal for clarifying just why it is that a team needs to form in the first place—in other words, the project's stated purpose.

▶ **Performance goals.** Projects offer the benefit of clearly defining the endeavor's missions and objectives, and they also offer the opportunity to clarify specific performance goals. These are often framed in terms of milestone attainment, executed deliverables, and the successful meeting of identified quality standards. There may be no substitute for a team having a meaningful purpose, but the way to turn this purpose into action is through establishment of performance goals consistent with preset quality performance standards. Project teams are good models for groups in which our model applies because project performance goals and quality standards—and how they will be measured—tend to be articulated clearly and in advance. They become explicit targets for project teams to understand, meet, and hopefully exceed together.

▶ **Approach.** Projects are guided by project plans and schedules, which are management tools to document an approach to getting the work done. But in our view, project planning is not, in and of itself, a habit of highly effective teams. A project plan is certainly necessary, as it outlines an approach to project completion. But it does not drive team excellence nearly as fundamentally as the approach team members take to their team roles, to their understanding of the team itself, and to the clients for whom the team was created. A project offers a structure for a team approach, and then it is up to the team leader and its members to understand and, more importantly, to share an approach that offers the best opportunity for success. The fact is that any group or team can develop plans, but it can not dictate how well team-based relationships form. The ideal project approach combines planning with the more relationship-focused efforts that help ensure project success.

▶ **Mutual accountability.** Projects offer a framework for mutual accountability, built around the project plan. A project team is a good model for the type of teams in which our model applies because project plans tend to have milestones that the project team seeks to attain in a coordinated way. Projects carefully assign out responsibilities to different team members, which sets up a framework for mutual accountability. When achievement of a project milestone is at risk, the team knows it, because the project plan is in jeopardy. Accountability is built into the project planning, project communication, and project organizational structures. Project responsibilities are clear to the entire project team, as are understandings of the deleterious rippling effects that unmet responsibilities will have on coordinated milestone attainment.

In certain instances, our model applies to work teams as well. As Cohen and Bailey defined them, work teams are continuing work units responsible for producing goods or providing services. Their membership is typically stable, usually full-time, and well-defined. When work teams meet these criteria, the only substantive differences between them and project teams may be that project teams are often: a) time-limited; and b) explicitly focused on an external entity that contracted for or otherwise agreed to a specific project team to form and do some requested task. Work teams have a high level of interdependence, and they meet the other definitional elements of teams to which our model applies that are focused on having small numbers of people, highly complementary skills, highly common purposes and performance goals, and a high mutual accountability. The point is that work teams formed by an organization on its own behalf can have largely the same group dynamics as a time-limited project team with a clear set of customers or stakeholders. For purposes of clarity, however, we will use "project team" as our primary point of reference throughout the remainder of the book.

Defining team effectiveness

If we wish to present our views on the behaviors and attitudes of effective teams, we need to establish those that meet some acceptable and shared definition of effectiveness. The short answer is that a team is effective if it meets and exceeds the need(s) for which it was established. If the organization sponsoring the team thinks it did its work well, then it was an effective team. A multiplicity of outcomes matter to organizations that set up, operate, and analyze the work of teams, but all these outcomes tend to fall into one of three broad categories: (1) **performance effectiveness** as assessed by accepted or preset quantity and quality outputs; (2) **behavioral outcomes**, best tied to an external rating of satisfaction with the team's work and its methods, as judged by clients, customers, or other external stakeholders; and (3) **member attitudes**—effectiveness being, therefore, a somewhat subjective phenomenon tied not only to outputs and client satisfaction, but to members' sense that the team did its work well. Why is this very subjective category relevant to an objective analysis of team effectiveness? Well, think back to the original question we asked in the opening chapter of this book, about remembering a highly resonant team experience. When we have a model of team effectiveness in our minds, from prior experience, we have a model to emulate. Member attitudes about their team experience matter to organizations, because the resonant experience reinforces the value of teamwork to the members themselves. This is valuable to organizations, because it motivates members' interest to join and participate in future teams. It also provides an ability to share with future teammates the factors that increase the likelihood that the team will be a positive and productive experience for them all.

Examples from each of these "team effectiveness" categories are shown on the following page.

Figure 1: Team Effectiveness

Performance, Outputs	Behavioral Outcomes	Member Attitudes
More volume (more output) **High efficiency** (more done in less time) **Higher productivity** (more done with least amount of dedicated resources) **Better quality** (better products or services)	**Higher customer satisfaction** (met/ exceeded client expectations) **Better communication** (interactions and information-sharing were beneficial) **More creativity and innovation** (new, valuable ideas were generated) **Better attendance/ participation** (members were fully involved)	**Sense of cohesiveness** (felt togetherness) **Sense of involvement** (felt they were part of the team's work and contributed to its outcomes) **Sense of pride** (felt the team was effective) **Sense of shared identity** (related well to the team)

There might be a tendency to focus only on performance output-related results when considering the factors involved in team effectiveness. But research and our own empirical observations of teams show that more behavioral and attitudinal results are equally, if not more, important.

The ascendancy of project and work teams

The fact is that the relevance, importance, and overall value of project and work teams are far greater now than ever before. The evidence for this is compelling. In their review of the growing importance of teams, Cohen and Bailey noted a range of studies that document this industrial reality. For example, research they cited showed that 82 percent of companies with 100 or more employees report that they use teams, and in examining data on 56,000 U.S. production workers, one of the most common skills required by new work practices was the ability to work as a team. Now, in an increasingly service sector-oriented economy, organizations are turning to teams to implement best practices and to manage their client engagements.

The notion of working solely for a single boss within highly defined departmental and divisional structures is becoming rather antiquated. Nowadays, one is far more likely to work for, and be accountable to, many different individuals or project managers, in addition to a direct line supervisor who assumes more administrative management responsibilities. In many instances, it is the project manager who observes, directs, guides, and coaches one's work performance, even if the project manager is not the individual's organizational supervisor. Project and work teams are often the hub of the organization's day-to-day functioning, the group around which the new organization conducts business with its customers.

If a project team operates poorly, the enterprise suffers. It will need to redirect significant organizational resources to address the resulting problems. It seems as if the very paradigm of modern organizational inefficiency has changed—an inefficient company is not one with excess, unproductive layers, or one that is behind the technology curve, as was the case not so many years ago. In most instances, the fat is gone from the modern organization, and companies disappear rapidly when they fail to innovate to meet client demands. With most companies already pared down to raw muscle and embracing the realities of a dynamic global marketplace, the fundamental success strategy is built around doing far more with far less. And the way in which an enterprise's human capital is best leveraged is highly contingent on the strategic development and effective operation of client-focused project teams. The enterprise continues to need individual skills and competencies, but these aptitudes now are often best deployed within a team context. Teams are the nexus for business activity in the contemporary business operation, and demonstrating effective teamwork is the Holy Grail of the modern enterprise. If your organization's future is tied largely to success in delivering project-based outcomes to customers, then there may be no better investment it can make for the future than to develop strategies to optimize teamwork throughout the projects that anchor the enterprise's operations.

Team effectiveness research

Empirical research on team effectiveness shows interesting findings. One study, by Hye-Ryun Kang, Hee-Dong Yang, and Chris Rowley in *Human Relations*, looked into whether software development teams in Korea were more effective if they had a shared mental model (SMM), or if they had shared demographics. SMM is a theoretical construct about shared cognitions on the team, similar to those that underlie the concept of a collective mind. SMM is reflective of shared expectations about tasks and teammates. Shared demographics are more about common education, departments, age, ancestry, and the like. The researchers found that SMM (in other words, shared thinking with teammates about how to go about a task in order to get good results) was more important than shared personal demographic characteristics, in anticipating that the team would be effective. Put another way, what matters less to team effectiveness are relationship factors tied to demographically driven social attraction or affinity between people, and what matters more are the team members' ability to share common ideas and performance expectations—to "get on the same page," as it were.

There have been numerous studies about team effectiveness, looking into a range of variables and team characteristics. In 1997, Cohen and Bailey performed a review of a broad set of team effectiveness studies in organizations, and their summary included these findings about the universal aspects of team effectiveness that are consistently supported throughout the research literature:

1. The type of team matters for the determinants of effectiveness. For example, studies of project teams examine external processes and have found that they matter for performance effectiveness. Perhaps, the researchers found, there should be different models of effectiveness for different types of teams.

2. The performance and attitudinal benefits from self-directed teams are superior to those from parallel teams.

3. Group cohesiveness is positively related to performance.

4. Team members tend to rate the team's performance high if the team has engaged in healthy internal processes, such as collaboration and resolution of conflict.

Based on these overall summary findings, it is likely that if a learning model is able to impact project team cohesiveness and healthy internal processes, then it will also impact project team effectiveness. Our 6 Habits model is focused precisely on these team cohesiveness and healthy internal process factors.

CHAPTER 3

Understanding How Teams Develop

...the interrelations among the many parts of the group and the variables that influence group process almost defy comprehension. —D.R. Forsyth

Teams are groups. In fact, assuming you haven't noticed it already, we use the terms *team* or *teams* rather interchangeably with the terms *group* or *groups*. Groups are brought together for a range of purposes in our society—behavior fueled in part by the simple reality that humans are social beings, with a need to bond and form relationships with others in order to accomplish things and lead a satisfying life. Effective organizations—larger groups that typically form smaller teams to perform work—leverage their understanding of the dynamics and natural phenomena that occur in groups to their benefit. Companies know that effective teamwork is both performance-boosting and morale-boosting. Effective teams produce more, and they make people feel a stronger connection to their larger group identity, at the organizational level. Consequently, an organization's team-building strategy needs to be mindful of and control variables that influence the formation of group identity. In fact, the formation of group identity develops along a common and well-understood group development continuum.

Stages of group development

When a team is identified by an organization to do some project or work, members begin to develop, maintain, and manage the relationships with other members and the team itself. Members understand that participation on the team is an intrinsic part of performing one's job. More often than not, if one does not accept and begin relating to a team to which one has been assigned, one's overall job performance ratings will suffer. The same principle holds true for teams composed of different companies. When a project team crosses organizational lines, excellent team performance promotes the likelihood that the prime contractor will want to do business again with the subcontractors who performed so well on a previous project. So there is an instrumentality to teamwork, driven by economic self-interest. Organizations expect and require staff to function well on project teams, where so much of the company's success is at stake. Conversely, when individuals demonstrate difficulties on team assignments, their usefulness to their supporting organization becomes limited.

But there are other, highly potent group dynamics that influence behaviors as teams develop. Again, humans are social as well as economic beings, and when we form groups to accomplish work together, certain emotionally laden phenomena occur. There is, in essence, a social psychology to group development. Understanding more about social psychology is quite useful in understanding how teams build through certain phases.

Formal research on organizational groups began with the experimental studies of small work groups in an electrical factory in Hawthorne, Illinois by F.J. Roethlisberger and W.J. Dickson. This "Hawthorne Experiment" occurred during the economic boom of the 1920s and concluded at the height of the Depression in the 1930s. The goal was to discover how changes in working conditions might lead to increased productivity. In the early stages of the Hawthorne research, workers mostly ignored changes in their working conditions, and refused to increase productivity—perhaps manifesting a concern that more productivity would create a need for fewer workers at the plant. When the experiment was moved into a separate room, and the workers gradually became friends with the experimenters, they sometimes increased production even when conditions, such as the amount of lighting, were reversed and made worse. H. Arrow, J.E. McGrath, and J.L. Berdahl discovered early that groups can develop their own social norms independent of the external environment. This led to the human relations school of management, as practitioners interpreted the Hawthorne results to show that if management personnel took a personal interest in workers, the workers would respond by producing more.

Later reanalysis of the Hawthorne data, by Walter Wardell, discovered several flaws in the experiment, but there was general agreement that the group itself has the power to self-organize and develop in unpredictable ways because of the complex interaction of so many variables.

Just before the Second World War, social psychologist Kurt Lewin and others designed more controlled experiments to test the effects of leadership style on group behavior. They found that different styles of leadership—authoritarian, laissez-faire, or democratic—generated different group cultures, independent of the characteristics of the members. The research team used the same groups and rotated the same leaders among them, so the independent variable (the only aspect that changed) was that the leaders systematically changed their style of leadership. Each different style of leadership produced quite different behaviors, group cohesion, and morale. Authoritarian leaders, who put the most emphasis on order, generated the most production in the short run, as long as the procedures and outcome were repetitive. However, individual morale was very low, although group cohesion could be high if members united against the dictatorial leader. Laissez-faire leaders had the least organized groups, which tended to be quite chaotic, and all three dependent variables—production, morale, and cohesion—were very low. Democratic leaders, situated midway between the other two leadership styles, had a slightly lower output than dictatorial styles—at least at first—but these groups demonstrated higher cohesion and morale. Very significantly, *the product of the democratically led groups was greater group creativity.*

The implication of both the Hawthorne studies and the work by Lewin was that although outside leaders could influence group culture indirectly, no one could directly force groups to obey, without negative consequences. In particular, creativity could not be forced, only encouraged.

One of the most influential theories of group development and progression in teams and organizations was developed by Bruce Tuckerman in 1965. It is a theory that resonates even today, 40-plus years after it was first presented. His "Forming-Storming-Norming-Performing" model of group development is an elegant and helpful explanation of team development psychology and behavior.

Tuckerman's model explains that as a team develops maturity and ability, relationships establish and morph based on issues such as trust and interdependency. The group development progression that Tuckerman postulated includes the following phases:

1. Forming
2. Storming
3. Norming
4. Performing

Stage 1: Forming

Characteristics of this stage:

▶ High dependence on leader for guidance and direction.

▶ Little agreement on team goals other than those received from leader.

▶ Individual roles and responsibilities are unclear.

▶ Leader must be prepared to answer lots of questions about the team's purpose, objectives, and external relationships.

▶ Processes are often ignored.

▶ Members test tolerance of system and leader.

▶ Leader is more directive.

Stage 2: Storming

Characteristics of this stage:

▶ Decisions don't come easily within the group.

▶ Team members vie for position as they attempt to establish themselves in relation to other team members and the leader, who might receive challenges from team members.

▶ Clarity of purpose increases but plenty of uncertainties persist.

▶ Cliques and factions form and there may be power struggles.

▶ The team needs to be focused on its goals to avoid becoming distracted by relationships and emotional issues.

▶ Compromises may be required to enable progress.

Stage 3: Norming

Characteristics of this stage:

▶ Agreement and consensus forms among the team, who respond well to facilitation by leader.

▶ Roles and responsibilities are clear and accepted. Big decisions are made by group agreement.

▶ Smaller decisions may be delegated to individuals or small teams within the group.

▶ Commitment and unity is strong.

▶ The team may engage in fun and social activities.

▶ The team discusses and develops its processes and working style.

▸ There is general respect for the leader, and some leadership is shared by the team.

▸ Leader plays a facilitating and enabling role.

Stage 4: Performing

Characteristics of this stage:

▸ The team is more strategically aware, and knows clearly why it is doing what it is doing.

▸ The team has a shared vision and is able to stand on its own feet with no interference or participation from the leader.

▸ There is a focus on over-achieving goals, and the team makes most decisions with regard to criteria agreed with the leader.

▸ The team has a high degree of autonomy.

▸ Disagreements occur, but now they are resolved within the team positively, and necessary changes to processes and structure are made by the team.

▸ The team is able to work toward achieving the goal, and also to attend to relationship, style, and process issues along the way.

▸ Team members look after each other.

▸ The team requires delegated tasks and projects from the leader.

▸ The team does not need to be instructed or assisted.

▸ Team members might ask for assistance from the leader with personal and interpersonal development.

▶ Leader assumes a far more hands-off, delegation role to allow team members to perform in their team role.

Tuckerman's own synopsis of his Forming-Storming-Norming-Performing model included this description:

Groups initially concern themselves with orientation accomplished primarily through testing. Such testing serves to identify the boundaries of both interpersonal and task behaviors. Coincident with testing in the interpersonal realm is the establishment of dependency relationships with leaders, other group members, or preexisting standards. It may be said that orientation, testing, and dependence constitute the group process of *forming*.

The second point in the sequence is characterized by conflict and polarization around interpersonal issues, with concomitant emotional responding in the task sphere. These behaviors serve as resistance to group influence and task requirements and may be labeled as *storming*.

Resistance is overcome in the third stage in which in-group feeling and cohesiveness develop, new standards evolve, and new roles are adopted. In the task realm, intimate, personal opinions are expressed. Thus, we have the stage of *norming*.

Finally, the group attains the fourth and final stage in which interpersonal structure becomes the tool of task activities. Roles become flexible and functional, and group energy is channeled into the task. Structural issues have been resolved, and structure can now become supportive of task performance. This stage can be labeled as *performing*.

Highly effective teams understand these group dynamics and group development sequencing, and they appreciate the emotional consequences of each stage. Emotional resistance to subsuming one's self-interest to that of a group's interest is a characteristic of the first two stages. The supremacy of relationships characterizes the final two stages. A fifth stage, *adjourning*, which Tuckerman added to his model in 1971, reflects the human emotional need to achieve closure, especially after relationships have become so vibrant and team interdependence has been so powerful. Humans in groups form strong relationships, and a stage is needed that accounts for the psychological impact and needs that exist during team separation.

The implication of this group development model is that these phases show individuals moving from self-interest to group integration, making the internal and interpersonal transformation to comprehend that the team is an entity to which to relate. Additionally, teams offer wonderful opportunities for members to self-actualize and express their own identity through emotional resonance with others during a team experience.

Teams can "Form and Storm" for hours, days, or even months, before they surrender themselves to the Norming phase. Assuming Tuckerman's model applies, the implied secret of highly effective teams lies in the answer to an obvious related question: How might teams anticipate the resistance of the first two stages, and move through it and jump start themselves to the Norming and Performing phases? Assuming that the desired outcome for the team is high levels of performance, the team needs to get to the Norming and Performing stage as soon as possible. The six habits of highly effective teams are instrumental in establishing a climate in work groups that set the stage for more rapid high performance.

Alan Drexler, Ph.D., and David Sibbet, Ph.D., spent many years refining a comprehensive model of team performance that shows various predictable stages involved in creating and sustaining high-performance teams. The Drexler/Sibbet Team Performance Model illustrates team development in seven stages: four to create the team, and three to describe levels of performance. Their group development model is described as follows:

Stage 1: Orientation

Question: **Why am I here?**

When team members have resolved the issues of this stage, they have:

▶ Purpose

▶ Personal fit

▶ Membership

Stage 2: Trust building

Question: **Who are you?**

When team members have resolved the issues of this stage they have:

▶ Mutual regard

▶ Forthrightness

▶ Spontaneous interaction

Stage 3: Goal clarification

Question: **What are we doing?**

When team members have resolved the issues of this stage they have:

▶ Explicit assumptions

▶ Clear, integrated goals

▶ Identified roles

Stage 4: Commitment

Question: **How will we do it?**

When team members have resolved the issues of this stage they have:

▶ Shared vision

▶ Allocated resources

▶ Organizational decisions

Stage 5: Implementation

Question: **Who does what, when, and where?**

When team members have resolved the issues of this stage, they have:

▶ Clear processes

▶ Alignment

▶ Disciplined execution

Stage 6: High performance

Question: **Wow!**

When team members have resolved the issues of this stage they have:

▶ Flexibility

▶ Intuitive communication

▶ Synergy

Stage 7: Renewal

Question: **Why continue?**

When team members have resolved the issues of this stage, they have:

▶ Recognition

▶ Change mastery

▶ Staying power

Other theories of group development stemming from studies of very unstructured groups (which tend not to apply in the workplace) show a somewhat similar process of moving from phases of chaos to phases of harmony. So it seems as if the general theme of group development that can be applied to teams is this: Just forming a team, declaring its purpose, and assigning roles to members does not develop a team. A team develops on its own, based in part on leader strategies and in part on the members' readiness to move through its initial resistance toward a stage of social integration that facilitates team performance. All of these issues have implications for the habits we will describe in this book. In some ways, our habits are countermeasures to the difficulties different people have in forming a common culture, and in becoming cohesive. Let's discover exactly what the components of this model include.

CHAPTER 4

The 6 Habits of Highly Effective Teams

Simplicity is the ultimate sophistication.
—Leonardo da Vinci

The fact is, as Susan Cohen and Diane Bailey discovered, that team habits directly influence outcomes. When an organization takes on the challenge of

determining which skills it must develop in order to get to the next level, the selections it makes are strong reflections of the corporate culture. An organization's attitudes and approaches to learning tell a lot about how it conducts business. Nowadays, with the rapid pace of change and global competitiveness impacting its future viability, the enterprise is likely to have learning strategies that reflect an emphasis on performance, efficiency, client satisfaction, and urgency. But in the end, training is fundamentally a "people strategy." Its aims are to:

▶ **Add to peoples' competencies.** Companies cannot waste valuable time and resources on anything but skills they *need* in their workforce in order to compete effectively in the marketplace and to satisfy demanding customers.

▶ **Develop potential in people,** to optimize the organization's human capital and leverage this human capital with a focus on now and the future.

▶ **Invest in the future.** The premise of a training "investment" is that it will yield a return, achieve real results, and endure. The challenges today may be slightly different than the challenges tomorrow, but many skills learned today will be as applicable in the future as they are today.

The 6 Habits of Highly Effective Teams model we present in this book, similar to the 6 Habits of Highly Effective Bosses model we presented in our last book, is developed with these realities of the learning requirements of contemporary business in mind. The learning strategies that drive our model's approach to team skill development are derived from a focus on performance, efficiency, customer satisfaction, and urgency. These six habits are most definitely not all you'd ever need to know about team-building and teamwork. Frankly, having such a goal would be far too overwhelming anyway. Our model is geared to bringing about real results in real teams, and in real time.

Our approach is more practical than academic. It emphasizes exercises and explicit understandings rather than inferred actions from anecdotal representations. It focuses on elements of team effectiveness rather than recognitions of team dysfunction. We know people are busier now than ever before, and that learning must be tied closely to short-term, here-and-now performance improvement. There are no tricks or gimmicks in our model; indeed, the principles are tried and true. Our learning model takes the approach that there is a great deal of value in advocating a very short, but targeted, list of highly essential work skills, which members can learn and apply with the understanding that, "If I acquire these competencies, I am well on my way to jump-starting my group's success and my personal effectiveness in a team setting."

Once again in this book, as in our previous efforts, we employ a pyramid shape to convey the essence of the model. Pyramids have "staying power," as does our 6 Habits model. The Sphinx and other pyramids have been around for ages and ages, and the skills in our model, similarly, will never go out of style as long as people work together in team-based settings. Also, there is a process implied by the pyramid structure, in which the bottom layer is the foundation, the next layer builds on the foundation layer, and the smallest level is at the top, where the final brick of the structure is laid, conveying a kind of cumulative, capstone effect. Additionally, with six parts of the structure, the pyramid shape provides a sense of symmetry to the model, moving from three to two to one, reaching the top of the pyramid, where new heights are achieved! Models need symmetry as well, to convey a sense of order and rationality.

The figure on the following page presents the 6 Habits of Highly Effective Teams model graphically.

Figure 2: 6 Habits of Highly Effective Teams

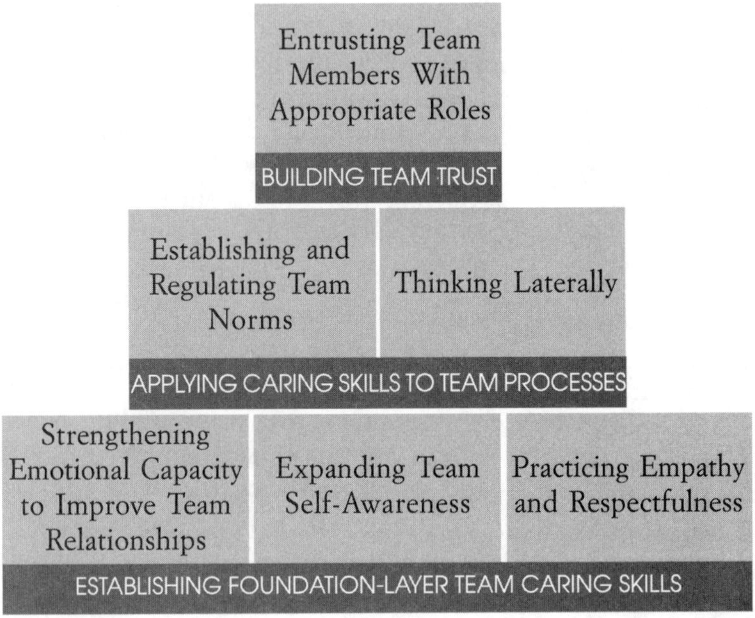

Entrusting Team
Members With
Appropriate Roles

BUILDING TEAM TRUST

Establishing and
Regulating Team
Norms

Thinking Laterally

APPLYING CARING SKILLS TO TEAM PROCESSES

Strengthening
Emotional Capacity
to Improve Team
Relationships

Expanding Team
Self-Awareness

Practicing Empathy
and Respectfulness

ESTABLISHING FOUNDATION-LAYER TEAM CARING SKILLS

Our use of the term *habits* in this model implies several of its important intrinsic features. If one was to say, "I am in the habit of" doing something, what does that mean? Habits are characterized by their:

1. **Frequency:** behaviors don't meet the definition of being "habits" if they are rarely manifested.

2. **Engrained nature:** a habit is a behavior that has become an integral part of one's common behavior pattern.

3. **Physical or psychological reward(s):** even "bad habits" reinforce some bodily or emotional need. Healthier habits are those that have produced the desired positive effect, and thus are worth repeating.

4. **Instinctive quality:** habits are performed without much forethought or extensive decision-making. If an action takes that much consideration, it is a better described as a reasoned choice, not a habit. Once an original reasoned choice gets repeated, again and again, it is no longer a selective behavior, but a more habitual behavior.

These characteristics of habits are consistent with how we wish our skill-building model to be perceived by the prospective habit-former. The behaviors we advocate need to be performed repetitively and frequently, engrain themselves in the team culture, reward and reinforce members (and the team itself) in their pursuit of project goals, and become almost second nature to teams. Indeed, it is when these skills become true team habits that the desired positive effects are most powerful.

Intentionally, there are no hard borders between the six habits we advocate. This conveys the sense that one habit easily blends with the others. Indeed, as you read our explanations of different habits, you will notice significant redundancies and overlaps among them. The model is integrated, it builds on itself, and skill development in one habit potentiates efforts to develop skills in another. We view this substantial overlap among the habits as a strength of our model. *Our habits work together—not unlike members of an effective team.* Each habit is distinct and has specific, individual qualities, just as a team member has. But the essence of a team is that individual entities complement each other. Our "team of habits" works together, creating team synergies that raise the effectiveness of the overall group when they are combined with each other.

PART II

CHAPTER 5

Habit #1:
Strengthening Emotional Capacity to Improve Team Relationships

While having the physical resources to do the job [is] important, so are the resources to deal with the emotion on the team....
—Elizabeth Christine Stubbs

Superior relationship skills drive a team's effectiveness. This truism is as universal and fundamental as any in organizational psychology. Anyone who has ever participated in any type of group project within an organization knows that success and morale are heightened when team members relate well with each other. Conversely, teams can be downright dysfunctional when members' relationship skills are absent, flawed, misdirected, untrusting, or not synchronized in any meaningful way.

Let's begin by getting very specific. Relationships clearly matter a great deal in effective teams, so how do these relationships form and strengthen? Where should a team's relationship skills be focused? The fact is that there are three distinct sets of interconnected relationships that pertain to truly superior performance within organizational project teams:

1. **Members' relationships to each other** within the team context (in other words, within the context of why the team exists; its purposes and goals). This includes the relationship of members to the team leader.

2. **Members' and team leaders' relationship to the team itself,** to the whole rather than the individuals who comprise it. Developing, managing, and maintaining this relationship to the team itself requires an understanding and acceptance of a group identity.

3. **Team relationships to external groups,** such as clients, suppliers, or various stakeholders.

Figure 3: Team Relationships

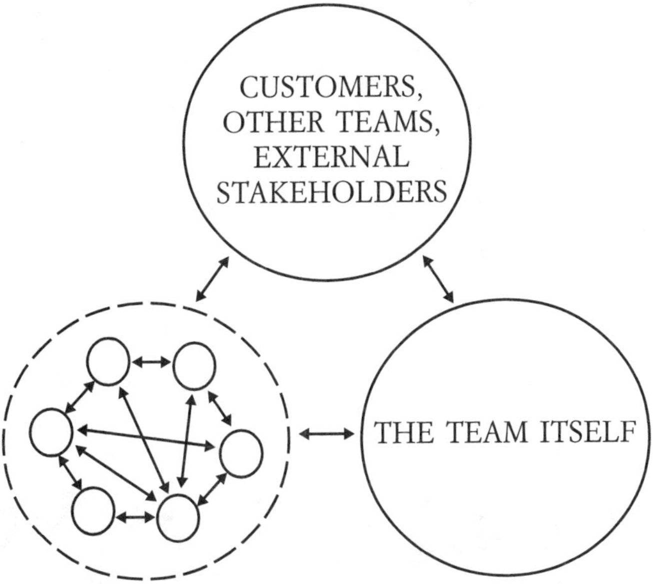

Is there a priority order to these three interconnected relationships? Does one matter more than the other two? The answer is that they all matter, concurrently, and always. But teams need to have the ability to identify when a particular relationship needs the most attention. Relationships are emotionally driven phenomena, and relationship management within a team is an emotional skill. Teamwork requires the emotional flexibility to adapt to the relationship imperatives of working within a group effort, as different circumstances dictate. In essence, the team itself needs to develop an "emotional intelligence." Teams need to build the capacity to be smart about the emotional aspects of managing their essential and interconnected relationships.

Based on the publications and work of Daniel Goleman and others about emotional intelligence (EI), there is now wide acceptance that people who demonstrate a certain set of emotional competencies advance more in their careers and are generally more successful in their social roles (for example, as relationship partner, parent, friend, community member) than those who exhibit lesser levels of these competencies. Goleman's model of emotional intelligence identifies four quadrants, reflecting behaviors that demonstrate awareness and management skills applied to oneself and to others:

Figure 4: Major Aspects of Goleman's Model of Emotional Intelligence

	SELF	RELATIONSHIP
A W A R E N E S S	▶ Emotional self-awareness ▶ Accurate self-assessment ▶ Core beliefs and values known ▶ Self-confidence	▶ Empathy ▶ Organizational awareness ▶ Service orientation ▶ Awareness of "political" currents
M A N A G E M E N T	▶ Stress management ▶ Self-control ▶ Drive to achieve ▶ Adaptability ▶ Optimism	▶ Conflict management ▶ Building instrumental bonds ▶ Developing potential in others ▶ Influence/persuasion ▶ Catalyst for change

Although the implications of demonstrating higher EI are well documented for individuals and organizational leaders, the concept of a team or group having higher or lower levels of EI is a relatively new one. Can a group of people—a team, as an entity unto itself—demonstrate emotional intelligence? Can a group be smart about its mood, its behavior, its emotions? There is a growing body of research that demonstrates not only that groups can manifest emotional intelligence, but that when they do, they perform more successfully.

In their article, "Building the Emotional Intelligence of Groups," which appeared in the Harvard Business Review, coauthors Vanessa Urch Druskatt and Steven B. Wolff present factors that drove the success of teams at IDEO, a prominent Midwestern industrial design firm.

> How does IDEO…ensure that its teams consistently produce the most innovative products under intense deadline and budget pressures? By focusing on its teams' emotional intelligence—that powerful combination of self-management skills and the ability to relate well to others.

They cite examples of EI at work at IDEO:

▶ A project leader notices a designer's frustration over a marketing decision and initiates negotiations to resolve the problem.

▶ During brainstorming sessions, participants pelt colleagues with soft toys if they prematurely judge ideas.

▶ The teams regularly assess the groups' strengths, weaknesses, and modes of interaction.

In research for her doctoral thesis at Case Western University, Elizabeth Christine Stubbs found that there was a relationship between a team leader's emotional intelligence and the team's EI norms. Additionally, her studies confirmed that a team leader's emotional intelligence affects team level emotional competence and team performance through the development of what Druskat and Wolff refer to as Emotionally Competent Group Norms. Thus, a leader's emotional intelligence can potentially impact how groups develop emotional capacity.

Indeed, "Team EI" is driven in part by the development and application of emotional competencies both by team leaders and by individual members of the team. But the fact is that teams with emotionally intelligent leaders and members are not automatically those that show emotional intelligence as groups. The foundation for the transfer of individual EI skills to team EI skills is, in part, volitional. It lies in the willingness—and perhaps, a type of emotional surrender—to frame issues from the perspective of the team rather than from pure self-interest. The key to applying individual EI skills to a team to which one belongs involves a shift from a focus on skills that promote awareness and management of oneself and others, to skills that promote awareness and management of the team's "self" and its others. This type of behavior is the essence of what a team needs to do to build its emotional capacity.

Consider the following case example:

Case Example

A university psychology department forms a committee of eight members to explore curriculum reform, based on student feedback that the curriculum is out of date and does not include more contemporary thinking about new psychological tests, trends, and innovative approaches to individual and group psychotherapy. Each of the eight members assigned to the committee project by the department chair has an earned doctorate in psychology. Individually, each of the committee members demonstrates superior emotional intelligence in interactions with students and with psychotherapy clients (each member has a private counseling practice in the community). If measured individual by individual, the aggregate EI of the group is extraordinarily high. But the team formed to pursue this curriculum reform project never developed any emotional intelligence of its own. Members never applied these skills to the team. Consequently, the committee quickly evolved into a totally dysfunctional group.

The obstacle to members applying their individual EI to this project involved a resistance to submit to a team effort to implement change. The tenured professors were highly resistant to recommending any substantive differences in the future curriculum, perhaps because they felt threatened by the fact that any new courses would fall outside their areas of expertise. Members developed factions, took rigid stances against the positions of other factions, postured intellectually with each other, and lost their focus on the team's documented purpose. The younger, untenured faculty on the committee eventually began to withdraw their energy and commitment to the team, seeing the committee as a waste of their time, an exercise in futility. The leader, who sided more with the tenured faculty, made tepid attempts to resolve the conflicts that undermined the group's efficacy, but he seemed to revel in the team's inertia because the consequence—no change—was what he sought. Eventually, the committee disbanded after half the members resigned from the group in disgust.

This team was dysfunctional not because the members did not have emotional intelligence, but because they did not apply their EI to each other, to the team itself, and to the team's clients—others at the university focused on academic affairs and curriculum development, as well as current and future students of the department. The committee members did not build the emotional capacity of the group they had joined. It turned out that, rather than exercising emotional intelligence in the overall committee, members reserved their relationship-building skills for the faction that sided with their self-motivated cause. The team never jelled because self-interest dominated, and group-oriented emotional intelligence skills were set aside in favor of an emphasis on self-preservation. While it is a useful starting point for leaders and team members to have superior EI, a team can only become emotionally intelligent when all members of the group apply relationship competencies to all other members of the team, to the team itself, and to the team's customers.

Consider the difference in the effectiveness of the team that applies emotional intelligence skills to another member, and to the team itself, for the purpose of promoting overall team harmony and effectiveness, as exemplified in the following case example.

Case Example

A proposal-writing team is told to change the proposal outline from which they had been working in one section, due to an executive sales manager's view that additional content is needed to ghost the competition. While the additional content is not specifically required in the client's request for proposal (RFP), the sales executive believes this section is the best place to provide important competitive information.

The individual who developed the proposal outline is taken aback by the sales manager's suggestion. The sales manager is not part of the team and will have little to do with the actual writing of the proposal itself. She objects to this idea, ostensibly due to her concern that this section has specific requirements in the RFP that must be addressed, and proposal space is highly limited. She expresses a fear that the new direction for this section will dilute the content needed to be compliant with the RFP requirements.

The proposal team members read her emotional reaction, which they view as driven by a "pride in ownership" in the outline she created. Members listen to her objections, but perceive defensiveness based on her shaken pride in having her diligently created outline changed at a late hour. In addition, members sense she is uncomfortable emotionally with the fact that such a senior executive found her outline to be less than perfect and missing strategic elements. Once this emotional assessment is made by other members of the team, several of them compliment her outline and the effort that went into developing it. They use anecdotal humor to share other instances when the same executive changed their hard work at the last minute. Upon feeling the team's support and understanding, and hearing how these types of higher-level interventions occur frequently and should not be taken so personally, the proposal outline creator joined in efforts to rejigger the outline to accommodate the suggested change.

There is much truth in this fundamental adage about groups: They are only as strong as their weakest link. Interpreted from an emotional intelligence perspective, this adage implies that effective groups understand that when an individual member is uncomfortable or not in sync with the group's norms or activities, it is best to address the problem right away. It is less a focus on resolving "weakness" than resolving a lack of resonance with team norms, expectations, processes, activities, and goals. Technical weaknesses can often be resolved through coaching, training, or adding new expertise to the team. It is the emotional issues that pose the most problems for teams, frequently in the form of a lack of synchronicity with the group processes. If an individual member is not resonating with others on the team for whatever reason, then team effectiveness inevitably will suffer. Thus, team interactions must confront individual members' emotional reactions that might sabotage the team's cohesiveness. At times, teams can advance the group's effectiveness by demonstrating emotionally intelligent relationship and management skills toward specific individuals within it. This is especially germane to interventions that are likely to promote team productivity and keep the project on track.

Effective teams make an effort to gauge their collective emotional temperature, and then react accordingly. How is this done when a team comprises individuals? The method involves framing problems, issues, and resulting discussions around the context of the group, rather than any one individual team member. At times, the challenge is to take the focus off specific content being considered (for example, a statement, a report, a piece of correspondence to the team) or what any one individual member shares verbally in the team setting. Rather, the focus is on assessing the emotions of the group itself. Group considerations reign; the team itself is perceived by members as a living, dynamic entity with an emotional temperature. Assuming this paradigm, interactions within the effective team change from statements such as:

I am confused by what I hear, and I think we need to consider the following.

to

There seems to be some uncertainty in the group, and this is frustrating us.

to

I am having trouble understanding the root cause of this problem.

to

The team does not seem to be drilling down to the root cause of the problem; let's assess what is getting in our way.

"I" statements are replaced with "team" or "we" statements. A simple change in communication approaches reinforces a team identity, and brings the group together as an entity itself, rather than a combination of individual members with a range of backgrounds and viewpoints. The "I" statements yield a need to help the individual speaker understand, but "we" and "the team" perspectives help define the group and focus the team on helping the group as a whole understand.

A case example clarifies this point:

Case Example

An IT project team for a government agency client meets to consider customer feedback data from routine user surveys. The team comprises a prime contractor and three subcontractors with substantial roles in performing the client's Statement of Work. In general, the feedback is glowing, with one exception: users complain about their ability to access e-mail accounts remotely. The network engineer responsible for establishing remote access systems, who works for one of the three subcontractors on the project, becomes defensive and sullen upon hearing this feedback in a quality meeting. It is clear he thinks this is not his fault, that there are other factors out of his control that prevent him from meeting client expectations. His body language shows a lot of frustration, and the team understands that he is feeling vulnerable, because no other user complaints were raised. Rather than putting the evidently frustrated and defensive network engineer on the spot about performance problems within his area of responsibility, individual members of the team point out to the entire team—not just to the defensive engineer—that "*we* have a problem." With this approach, the emphasis is placed on how all project systems are integrated and interconnected. Thus, any identified problem needs to be the focus not only of any single individual, but also of the overall team itself. Rather than asking the engineer in charge of remote access to assess the problem and report back to the team about potential fixes, the team forms an ad hoc problem-solving group with representation from all of the project's functional areas.

In essence, the interaction steers a wide berth away from blaming a single person or subcontractor for the customer-identified problem, and instead reinforces a critical group norm about shared performance responsibilities. By stating that this is a team problem to be solved by the team as a whole, the team interacts with itself, reinforces its group identity, and avoids intercompany disputes that might undermine the project team's cohesiveness. By framing the problem-solving in a team context, the group is able to promote an emotional atmosphere that avoids blame and works toward a productive, team-based solution.

This organizational case example shows not just individual members demonstrating good emotional awareness and relationship management skills, but also the team demonstrating these competencies within its problem-solving processes. The team has a client, the client has a problem, and therefore the team has a problem. Problem-solving activities are initiated with representation from all functional areas of the team, with an understanding that the entire project is an integrated team effort. The team becomes uncomfortable, not because an individual member is uncomfortable, but because the client is not satisfied with an element of the team's performance. *Greater emotional capacity in the team drove greater responsiveness to the client.* Therefore, teams need to direct relationship skills toward themselves and, by inference, toward their customers. In essence, by focusing on the team itself, all three interconnected team relationship imperatives are addressed: those that exist between individual members, within the team itself, and with the team's customers.

External relationship management by teams

Teams play an important role in building, maintaining, and managing customer relationships. An organization's success is highly contingent on its ability to satisfy—and hopefully delight—its customers. Without clients and the revenues they generate, the enterprise ceases to be viable. Although a particular relationship manager or point of contact may be the individual with corporate responsibility for managing a specific account or external relationship, client relationship management is often a team effort. Effective teams know where their bread is buttered. They understand that high client satisfaction means steady work, better job security, and opportunities for future projects with the same customer.

It is important for a team to grasp the notion that the interface between an entity that purchases products or services and the team that plays such a large role in providing the purchaser with the same, is a relationship. It can be a sterile, price-driven relationship, or it can become as close of a mutual partnership as two distinct, independent organizations or entities can have with each other. But it *is* a relationship between the two parties, with all of the associated opportunities, pitfalls, and emotional nuances that accompany any interdependent relationship.

A team needs emotionally intelligent relationship management skills to help ensure the highest levels of client satisfaction. What are the relationship issues at the heart of interactions between a team and its outside client(s), customer(s), and other stakeholders? When two organizations transact business with each other, there are a set of transcendent, overarching needs that clients expect their suppliers to meet, no matter the stage of the relationship. These can be referred to as the "meta-level relationship needs" of clients. An appreciation of these needs should be integrated into the fabric of the team's operations and processes. They need to guide the day-to-day priority-setting and decision-making within the team. It is incumbent on the team, the team leader, and all individual members to champion these client needs at all times.

CHEEARS in the team's ears

We have developed an easy-to-remember acronym for listing these seven meta-level relationship needs, of which all organizational teams should be aware: CHEEARS. Think of what you are likely to hear, from the client and from your firm's senior leadership, if your organization performs well in meeting these meta-level relationship needs! (Obviously we have taken liberties with the spelling of the word—a common device used by those of us in the acronym-building game! Think of combining the beginning and ending of the phrase, "CHEers in your EARS," creating CHEEARS.)

In any event, whether you make use of our memory-spurring acronym or not, being aware of and creating systems that address these seven meta-level relationship needs are imperative for the highly effective team.

Competence

Clients expect their suppliers to perform capably—period. They require that their suppliers—including all of the suppliers' team members who will participate on a project they are funding—demonstrate all the competencies that were outlined, described, or even implied to them when the contract or purchasing arrangement was finalized. The decision by a client to purchase a product or service through an external supplier, rather than choosing to produce or perform it in-house, involves the implicit preference to leverage the superior competencies that exist in the marketplace. The purchaser makes the assumption that the product or service it is buying involves competencies that it either cannot perform cost-efficiently on its own, or should not perform because an outside source is more appropriate (for regulatory or legal reasons). No matter how well a team establishes a bond with a client, it is the competent delivery of services that drives the business relationship.

At the core of the buyer-seller relationship is the seller's requirement to competently deliver what the client desires.

Questions to consider:

▶ What are your team's key competencies? How does the team feel about its competence level at this time?

▶ What quality assurance systems are in place to facilitate an ongoing, cost-effective assessment that your team delivers highly competent products or services?

▶ Are you measuring your team's competencies, and developing plans to build them within your organization's teams to an even higher level?

▶ Do your organization's teams have a full understanding of your organization's overall competencies? Also, does your team make an effort to asses and regularly feed back to the organization competencies that are in demand by particular clients?

Honesty/Integrity

When an agreement is reached to supply a purchaser with a product or service, the project team must be forthright about its ability to deliver, both in the near term and beyond. Then, during the delivery process, interactions with purchasers must remain honest, truthful, and representative of the team's commitment to keeping its promises. Teams cannot guarantee what they cannot deliver in order to win the business, and then hope they will be able to talk their way through or somehow sidestep the deception later. Solid client relationships are built on trust. A lack of honesty and/or any activity or communication that shows that the team is not committed to behaving with integrity is probably the most potent of relationship-killers. It is impossible for a client to be loyal to a vendor and the teams who represent this vendor when the team's behavior is not trustworthy.

Questions to consider:

▶ When your team makes mistakes, is the mistake promptly admitted to the client?

▶ If product delivery/service delays occur or are likely to occur, does the team own up to them and take responsibility?

▶ Does the team allocate resources in a way that places top priority on your team's ability to keep the promises it has made to clients?

Empathy/understanding client needs

This need is strongly tied to the skill of active, empathetic listening, which we will discuss in greater depth in Habit #3. Empathy is a skill that is "other-oriented," not selfish or self-serving. Clients want teams, and the organizations they represent, to make an effort to truly understand their industry and unique business challenges. How else can they create effective solutions for their clients, if they make little effort to understand their clients' concerns? The perception that teams hope to create is that they truly care about their client's issues—indeed, that the client's business issues are, in effect, the supplier team's issues too. Exhibit 1 shows the "Buy-Sell Hierarchy," reflecting how a client relationship can develop from more commodity-based selling to one that is an understanding-driven partnership. Reaching the top of this hierarchy, in which a true business partnership is developed between buyer and seller, is only possible when the organization—or more specifically, the team that does business with the client—has a full understanding about the client's challenges and issues.

Questions to consider:

▶ How does the team tune in to your client's current business issues?

▶ What resources are available to the team to get to know your client's business challenges even better?

▶ How much talking does your team and its members do in interactions with clients, and how much of the time do you spend asking questions and seeking first to understand—in other words, practicing empathy?

Figure 5: The Buy-Sell Hierarchy

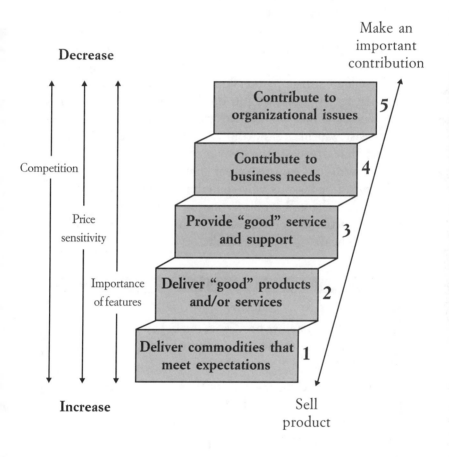

Easy to work with

This need is more subjective, and may fluctuate somewhat based not just on the nature of the project that the team performs, but also on the personalities of the key contact people on the client side. Being easy to work with is a function of a team's affirmative attitude that its clients should not face undue hassles or difficulties that may interfere with achieving desired outcomes. It is about creating user-friendly systems that facilitate a true partnership with clients. It is about being inclined to say, "Yes, we can do that," or at least, "Yes, I understand how that would help you—let me see how our team can assist you in getting those results you are looking for." Firms that are easy to do business with are flexible and accommodating, to the extent that they can be. They seek solutions, not reasons why something would not work. They realize that clients have little interest in the team's systems or the supporting organization's bureaucracy—the client's sole focus is always on getting results.

Questions to consider:

▶ What systems, processes, or behaviors could be improved to make your team easier to work with from a client's perspective?

▶ Are there any patterns or trends in the complaints your team fields from clients about efficiently getting the results the clients are looking for?

▶ How are special requests from clients handled? Does the message conveyed back to the client demonstrate an interest in being easy to work with?

Accessibility

Clients need to be able to reach their respective contacts at the supplier's team, to ask questions, receive updates, plan future interactions, and so on. Teams must be committed to systems that promote accessibility. This may include having voice mail systems that offer an ability to "zero-out" to a live administrative staff member or helpful operator, e-mail systems backed up by reliable servers, cell phones or other handheld electronic devices with reliable coverage and clarity of service, vacation planning that never leaves the client without a reliable contact on the team who can respond to urgent concerns, and management of staff turnover such that accessibility vacuums are not created when a key internal team member—especially one who was a leading client contact—leaves the organization.

Questions to consider:

▶ Are your team members equipped for full accessibility?

▶ How difficult would it be for a client to reach a "live" person on the team if he or she wished to?

▶ What kind of coverage exists when a key team contact is out of communication for many hours?

Responsiveness/follow-through

Even if clients find your team highly accessible, it is critical that client concerns brought to the team's attention be acknowledged and responded to. If a client has no problem getting through to your team, but then the issues that are raised are not attended to, the effort expended to be as accessible as possible is for naught. The meta-level relationship need is for the team to be responsive, to take the actions that must be taken—especially actions about which there has been mutual agreement. Once clients have been assured by your team that a task or action will be performed—any task, be it large and highly visible or small and seemingly mundane—they expect that it will get done. Figure 6 shows research findings about behaviors that "bother" or "impress" purchasers. At the top of the list of behaviors that are most impressive to buyers is the ability to follow up and follow through on what had been agreed to. Not surprisingly, a lack of follow-through is the most irksome of supplier behaviors.

Questions to consider:
▶ How does your team track items for which clients are expecting a response or follow-up?

▶ How does the team stay informed about follow-up items? Are team members empowered to assure that internal resources are properly deployed to respond to clients' needs?

▶ How does the team create mutual accountability to feel comfortable that client follow-through is occurring?

In *Key Account Management and Planning*, Noel Capon cites a study that identified a series of relationship issues that bother and impress clients, shown on the following page.

Figure 6: Behaviors That Bother and Impress Clients

BOTHER		IMPRESS	
Behavior	**Percent**	**Behavior**	**Percent**
Lack of follow-up	28%	Thoroughness, follow-through	78%
Lack of preparation for meetings	15%	Willingness to fight for client in own firm	59%
Cold calls	15%	Market knowledge/ willingness to share this knowledge	40%
Too pushy/ bad attitude	15%	Knowledge of own products	40%
Lack of product knowledge	11%	Imagination in applying products to clients' needs	29%
Dishonesty	7%	Preparation for sales calls	20%
Lack of knowledge of company's operations	6%	Diplomacy in dealing with client's operating departments	15%
Lack of market or industry knowledge	5%	Regularity of sales calls	9%
Not adhering to appointment times	5%	Technical education/ expertise	9%

Sharing information/communication

Solid business relationships (just as personal relationships outside work) are built on full and open communication between the parties. Purchasers have little tolerance for suppliers' teams who are cautious about the information they share, appear reluctant, or lack urgency in providing needed information on a regular basis. In general, the more information that is communicated, the better. Clients never want to feel as if they are in the dark with respect to the status of a project assignment, milestone, or deliverable. E-mail messaging makes communication easier these days, but relationships can become distant when all the information sharing is done through electronic means. It is important to have telephone conversations and in-person meetings regularly, to allow for a more personal and open exchange of information. These "live" interactions allow the team and its leader to ask questions and better understand the clients' needs.

Collaboration tools and other knowledge management technology, sometimes called "groupware," can assist the team in performing its information-sharing competence and activities. These software tools are designed to help people involved in a common task achieve their information-sharing goals. Also called "collaborative software," groupware is an evolving concept that is more than just multi-user software that allows access to the same data. Groupware provides a mechanism that helps users coordinate and keep track of ongoing projects together. When project team leaders prioritize information-sharing with all members of the team—as well as the client's project leaders—through shared groupware access and knowledge-sharing activities, they demonstrate a commitment to this relationship management principle.

Questions to consider:

▸ What means does your team use most to communicate with clients: e-mail? Telephone calls? In-person visits? Documents/written correspondence? Other?

▸ What information would you be reluctant to share with a client? Why?

▸ What feedback has your team received about how well it shares key information with clients?

When teams use the CHEEARS model as a foundation for the norms they establish and by which they abide, they are well-positioned to strengthen their customer relationships. And because these are "meta-level" relationship-building factors, they apply to relationships within the team, as well. Effective, cohesive teams demonstrate all the CHEEARS principles with each other.

Operating principles of relationship management

From research done on team-client relationship-building, we have developed a set of recommended principles to guide teams and the organizations they represent in the role they play with clients. These seven operating principles of team-client relationship management should blend together into a kind of guiding mantra for teams as they go about implementing their client relationship management strategies.

The seven operating principles of team-client relationship management

1. Teams must always add value.

The "Buy-Sell Hierarchy" shown earlier conveys how a seller can move from a commoditized, price-sensitive, highly competitive position with a client to one that is more of a partnership, by understanding the client's issues and always adding value. Broadly speaking, there are three areas in which the project team can add value:

1. **Functional:** The value is in the solution to a tangible or operational problem the client has.

2. **Economic:** The value is to increase the purchaser's volume of business, revenues, or income; or ways to reduce the purchaser's operating or opportunity costs.

3. **Psychological:** The value encompasses factors within the buyer's psyche, such as risk reduction, peace of mind, comfort in a relationship, pride in doing the right thing, or other factors not tied to a functional or economic need.

2. Teams must always add value before reducing prices or fees.

We have reviewed how value-added relationships actually reduce price sensitivity (the more value you offer your clients, the less price matters to them). When price or fee reductions are discussed, teams need to explore alternatives that reinforce that the relationship developed with the team's organization is extremely valuable in and of itself. When clients take the position that the relationship will only be enhanced by reduced prices or fees, then the seller must acknowledge that the relationship is reverting to a more commoditized buyer-seller interface.

There are many "currencies" that can be leveraged to add value to clients, and preclude the need to reduce prices or fees. Here is a brief summary of these types of value-enhancing currencies:

▶ **Expanding the client's vision:** Helping the client see the larger significance of the seller's features in terms of the unit, the organization, customers, or society.

▶ **Excellence:** Offering a buyer the chance to do important things exceptionally well.

▶ **Moral/ethical correctness:** Offering the chance to do what is right by a higher standard than efficiency.

▶ **Adding resources:** Lending resources, such as manpower, space, or equipment, which will assist the client in getting important things done.

▶ **Assistance with unwanted tasks:** Volunteering to take on chores or tasks that the client finds loathsome, irritating, or tangential to its primary role. The willingness to do so can add considerable value to the relationship, from the gratitude it engenders.

▶ **Cooperation:** Giving task support, providing quicker response time, approving something that a client wants approved, or aiding in implementation.

▶ **Information:** Providing industry-specific, organizational, competitive, or technical information or knowledge.

▶ **Advancement:** Performing in a way that highlights the client's skills, abilities, judgment, and so on, and paves the way for advancement opportunities.

▶ **Recognition:** Performing in a way that gets the client recognized by higher-ups or within the industry.

▶ **Visibility:** Offering products or services that make the client more visible.

▶ **Reputation:** Helping the client's reputation, such as being an innovator or quality leader.

▶ **Importance or belonging:** Helping clients reach a status that facilitates their inclusion in exclusive groupings to which they aspire.

▶ **Network/contacts:** Promoting access to influential individuals, potential customers, or industry/professional gurus.

▶ **Acceptance:** Providing closeness and friendship.

▶ **Personal support:** Backing clients up personally.

▶ **Understanding:** Listening and showing sincere caring for the client.

▶ **Self-concept:** Offering the opportunity to affirm the client's values and identity.

▶ **Challenge/learning:** Sharing tasks that increase the client's skills and abilities.

▶ **Ownership/involvement:** Letting others have ownership and influence.

▶ **Gratitude:** Expressing appreciation and indebtedness for assistance.

The message that teams need to stress to clients should be that their close business relationship has real, measurable value. This is evident when the client acknowledges that, "Working with your team makes my job easier," and/or, "The work your team performs makes our organization operate more efficiently and makes our organization's products and services more marketable." Clients are more likely to accept alternatives to price or fee reductions if suppliers are able to enhance their chances to look good within their organization or profession, and when they find it a pleasure and personally rewarding to work with the suppliers and teams who represent them.

Teams must add value in as many of the three fundamental areas—functional, economic, and psychological—as possible. Doing so is an investment in avoiding the prospect of having to expend resources to continuously fend off the competition, engage in bidding wars, or reduce marginal profits in order to keep the client's business.

A note on including the word *always* in relationship management principles one and two: Clients look for a consistent and unremitting relationship-building effort from suppliers' project teams. Every day offers another opportunity to impress the client with the value that doing business with your team holds. There are so many ways to add value, and so many currencies to spend in order to do so, that it is quite reasonable for clients to expect suppliers to constantly and persistently add value to the client's business.

3. Teams are the face of and fully represent their organization.

Clients expect that when they are interacting with their supplier's project team, they are discussing an issue or negotiating *directly* with the supplier organization itself. Teams must never set up a situation that makes it unclear to the client whether the team speaks for the organization it represents. Further, teams must avoid setting up a triangular relationship with the client—one that sets apart an executive, department, or different operational team within the enterprise as a third party with which negotiations will need to be held separately. Clients want a direct, uncomplicated, two-way, results-oriented relationship with the project teams with which it contracts. And the team is the personification of the firm's commitment to the client and to the client relationship.

4. Clients do not care about their suppliers' internal systems.

Teams need to be mindful that internal structures or bureaucracies within their organization that could be resistant to or offer an obstacle to finding a solution to a client's needs, are irrelevant to the client. It is wasteful and relationship-harming to try to explain these internal issues. Rather, the best strategy is to demonstrate to the client a firm commitment to finding appropriate solutions, and then to negotiate internally without the client's involvement. Do not drag the client into your internal turf wars, interdepartmental squabbles, or operational snafus. The client does not care about them. To the client, it is all about results.

5. Teams must never waste the client's time.

This issue was alluded to earlier in Table I, which lists the behaviors that impress and bother clients. Clients are busy, and your time with them is precious. Meetings need to be well-organized. Appointment times should be honored. The content of the interactions should add value. The team wants the client to have the opinion that after every contact with the team, the client will always learn something new or find itself closer to a valuable business goal. When clients give a team time from their busy calendars, the interaction needs to be focused and informative, leaving clients in a better position than they were before the interaction occurred. Conversely, time-wasting behavior is very perilous to client-team relationships. Teams need to be very cognizant of this, and prepare diligently for all client interactions.

6. Teams must spend time nurturing internal relationships.

This operating principle is a reminder that a team's relationship with clients is vitally connected to the relationships that are built within the team, and the relationship between the team leader or project manager and the team members. Project managers need to understand their clients' needs, but they will have great difficulty meeting these needs without being connected to the teams responsible for implementing client projects. A solid portion of a project manager's calendar needs to be spent within the team, nurturing the relationships that will make the project manager's interactions with a client successful. This internal work within the team is crucial in accomplishing three interrelated success factors for performing within a lead relationship management role:

1. Ensuring action and responsiveness to clients.

2. Ensuring internal commitment to the client's projects or programs.

3. Involving team members in relationship activities with the client.

Interestingly, research with lead client relationships or project managers shows that they tend to do less of this internal relationship-building than they do managing project tasks or understanding the client's business. But the message that excellent project managers understand is: "I cannot do it all alone. And if that is so, I need to be connected to others and gain their commitment to my client." The larger the project, the more team resources will need to be devoted to the contract. Thus, the need to spend time on internal relationships in order to manage key accounts becomes even more relevant. Clients can tell when there is a disconnect between the project manager and the team, and they can slowly lose faith in this manager if the disconnect persists.

7. Teams must make a team commitment to skill development and learning.

To always add value, teams need to be on the leading edge of trends in the industry, new technologies that could assist in meeting client needs, and personal skills that translate into better relationships with key client contacts. Clients admire project teams who share new knowledge with them. They also admire people or groups of people with whom they do business who have a propensity to learn, who look to advance their own knowledge base, who have an attitude that one is never too old or too experienced to stop learning new things. Ultimately, this principle is very much a part of the overall principle of *always adding value*. It is from constant skill development and learning that value-adding activities are performed well.

Clients are aware when a team's solutions are getting stale, redundant, or stagnant. They can sense when there is a lack of "fresh blood" in solution-finding by the team. Therefore, it is crucial to the team's performance to commit itself to self-improvement activities, to making a regular effort to develop professional and personal competencies that add value for the clients.

Summary

Although there is general acceptance of the value of emotional intelligence for leaders and individuals, the concept that teams can be emotionally intelligent is rather new. But research and practice are demonstrating that teams that build emotional capacity can manage their relationships better, and thus be far more effective.

Building emotional capacity is tied to understanding the concepts of emotional intelligence, and applying it to the group.

High EI individuals who do not leverage this skill for the benefit of the team can actually bring about team dysfunction.

Three sets of interconnected relationships need to be the focus of teams:

1. Members' relationships with each other.
2. Members' relationship to the team itself.
3. The team's relationship to external clients and stakeholders.

Building effective external relationships with clients and stakeholders requires understanding and establishing processes to meet the meta-level relationship needs of clients—CHEEARS!

▶ Competence
▶ Honesty
▶ Empathy/understanding client needs
▶ Easy to work with
▶ Accessibility
▶ Responsiveness/follow-through
▶ Sharing information/communication

Teams should heed the seven operating principles of team-client relationship management:

1. Teams must always add value.
2. Teams must always add value before reducing prices or fees.
3. Teams are the face of and fully represent their organization.

4. Clients do not care about their suppliers' internal systems.

5. Teams must never waste the client's time.

6. Teams must spend time nurturing internal relationships.

7. Teams must make a team commitment to skill development and learning.

CHAPTER 6

Habit #2:
Expanding Team Self-Awareness

Those final minutes are what keeps me a believer in good ol' Devils hockey. —A blogger at the NHL Direct Blog Site at *NHL.com*

Effective teams have an identity. When a team has an identity, team members and the team's clients are able to relate more to the team entity itself. A team's identity is driven less by its name (if it has one), or by individual identities of team members who comprise it, than by the following aspects that reflect a team's character:

▶ Its shared mission.

▶ Its values and the norms that stem from these values.

▶ Its competencies and strengths.

▶ The perceptions of those with whom it interacts.

How does a team build an identity? The answer is connected directly to the development of actions that build a team's self-awareness. Indeed, by dedicating time, resources, attention, and leadership activities in support of team identity-building, teams are able to establish, in essence, a team "self." Similar to the process of identity development in individuals, a team builds its sense of self around shared perceptions among team members that the group itself is a discrete, separate entity. In part, this process of establishing a team self is made easier by the fact that when individuals belong to a group, they derive at least a portion of their personal sense of self from the group. If a team to which one belongs helps form the individual's identity, it is logical that a team's identity is also a function of the team members' shared perceptions of what the team means to them. In this way, team identity is driven by individual members' need to develop their own sense of self based on their participation in a group activity. The habit of expanding team self-awareness is connected to the intrinsic connection people wish to have to valuable group experiences.

But the most salient factors in a team's ability to build a sense of self are not so psychodynamic; they are more cognitive, born out of extensive thinking about and dedication to self-awareness-building activities. They begin from the outset, in the team's Forming stage, and continue throughout the group's development. Team identity begins with concerted efforts by team leaders and members who understand the value of developing an understanding about what the team stands for, and what makes it a distinct group. The habit that highly effective teams have of expanding team self-awareness involves useful team-building methods aimed at forming and maintaining a sense of team identity. We will share both the methods and relevant team-building exercises that support these efforts to expand team self-awareness.

First, the team needs a name

Although the name of a project team may not necessarily describe the team's identity, a team name is valuable because team members, team leaders, and team clients are able to connect better to the team entity when there is a name or label to which to relate. Naming a team is similar to a marketing branding strategy: It provides a label around which the team can form its identity and build emotional resonance and interconnected relationships. Ideally, the name of the team should be congruent with its mission, purpose, function, or client. The purpose of naming a team is to convey these factors in a way that fosters an emotional attachment to the whole. But the name should not be trite or overly cute. We have seen enormous resonance with simple but positive labels for teams, such as "Flight" (a database development project team modifying an airline reservation system database) or "Studio" (a project to add software development office space). Or the name can simply be the acronym of the project title, which often ends up resembling a real word, such as TSTI (pronounced by team members as "testy") for Triangle Services Technology Improvement. When members of New Jersey's ice hockey team and its fans have a shared understanding of what "good ol'

Devils hockey" is, it has nothing to do with anything demonic! Rather, their identity is based on a shared perception that "Devils hockey" means hard work, opportunistic goal-scoring, defensive play, and great goaltending. The resonance of a group with its name is about the team's features—the characteristics that capture the team's essence. The name is less important than the perception of what the name means to itself, its members, and its constituents, but teams must have a name. This is a requirement of highly effective team-building.

Developing a mission statement

Developing a team mission statement is a useful exercise, early in the team formation process, to help the team clarify its purpose and common objectives. The statement should be clear, concise, and understandable. Team mission statements are outcome-oriented, not process-oriented. They also incorporate client factors; that is, they convey whom the team is serving. A team's mission is integrally connected to the concept that it exists not for itself, but to serve some external customer or customers.

A team's mission statement can be as simple as a single sentence long, and it should be no longer than three statements. Again, the more concise the team mission statement, the better. It should include factors of the team's purpose, structure, responsibility, and membership. A discussion to formulate a mission statement should gather ideas and guide the team in all activities it pursues. We encourage teams developing their mission statement to consider:

▶ Why is this team necessary?

▶ What objectives drive the team's efforts?

▶ Who benefits from effective work by the team?

▶ To what standards of performance excellence should the team aspire?

▶ What actions (verbs) exemplify what the team is all about?

The action verb should capture the essence of the actions taken by the team. For example, if the team is a service provider, then "provides" or "delivers" might be logical verbs to include in the mission statement. If it is a research team, verbs such as "explores," investigates," or simply "conducts leading-edge research" might capture the mission best. If the team is involved in management functions, then its mission statement verbs might include "administers," "plans," or "organizes."

Developing a team mission statement is a project team requirement—it is not optional. These statements should be developed, agreed to, endorsed by the larger organization, and then published. If the team works in a specific space, it is useful to post the team mission statement in a visible spot within a common area, such as a conference or break room. When the team, using its emotional intelligence, senses it is off course and expresses frustration about being adrift or out of focus, the best response by the team may be to simply revisit its mission statement. This self-awareness reinforcement action by the team can have profound effects on subsequent team decision-making and planning. The mission statement always reflects the overall direction of the team. If, for any reason, the mission statement no longer reflects what the team stands for, it needs to be reconsidered, reformulated, reapproved, and redistributed.

Clarifying the team's values

Values contribute to the team's norming process, which we will review in more depth in Habit #4. But as norms are about agreement to team attitudes, processes, and behaviors, team values are more about the group's underlying core beliefs. A team's self-awareness is built not only on mutual expectations about member behaviors, but also at a deeper level by the values that serve as the foundation for these behaviors. Team values beget team norms.

A team credo exercise is useful in clarifying team values. It asks members to reflect on and contribute to a consensus process of completing the sentence, "Our team believes...." Look at the chart on the following pages to see how the core beliefs of highly effective teams engender the norms that guide day-to-day team attitudes, processes, and behaviors.

Figure 7: Examples of Team Beliefs, Values, and Resulting Norms

Team belief/value	Team norms derived from this belief/value
To be effective, team members need to respect each other and the contributions each member makes to the team.	We listen to each other, without interrupting. We communicate openly and often. We maintain our assigned roles.
To be effective, a team needs to manage its time well.	We start and end meetings on time. Our meetings have agendas. We come prepared to meetings, with information or materials consistent with the agenda.
To be effective, teams need to engender creativity and innovation.	We encourage provocative ideas. We think laterally.
To be effective, teams need to trust one another.	We refrain from instant judgments, seeking first to understand. We empower members to perform their roles on the team.

	We delegate work to others on the team when doing so brings efficiencies and greater productivity.
To be effective, teams need to manage conflict.	We do not personalize conflict. We seek to differentiate any conflict (understand the respective positions in the conflict), then search for common ground. We channel all program reports through the project manager.
To be effective, the team needs to understand its client(s) and manage the client relationship.	We seek to always add value for our clients. We follow up actively and immediately on client requests and complaints. We take time to listen to and understand our clients' needs.

There are other values and associated norms of highly effective teams, but these examples provide a model for the connection between documenting team values and establishing team norms—a process so important in and of itself that it deserves its own designation as one of the six habits of highly effective teams (Habit #4).

In essence, developing a team credo is a method of expanding the team's self-awareness, and it is also a team emotional intelligence-building exercise. Because beliefs are strongly felt values by individuals, teams may need time together to understand and share them with each other in a team context. That is, teams may need time and experience together to feel comfortable with and better understand their team beliefs. Team beliefs may be slightly different than individual beliefs about team effectiveness. It is often appropriate for teams to begin, not with team credo-developing exercises, but with more straightforward norming efforts, to develop the behavioral expectations of members. Many norms are rather concrete and directive, such as those reflecting a need to manage time effectively. Being a bit more emotionally neutral, these types of norms are congruent with the team Forming or Orientation stages. But eventually, teams need to spend time developing their underlying beliefs, in the form of a team credo.

However, some teams are prepared and able to develop beliefs and norms together from the beginning. The decision to develop team norms first, and then revisit them in the context of subsequent team-building exercises once the team has developed more emotional capacity, or to determine its team norms immediately after discussing and documenting a team credo, is dependent in part on the extent of previous experience team members have with each other. The sequence is a decision that the project team leader needs to make, but values clarification by the team and the documentation of team norms are required respective elements of building an effective team. They are critical to team self-awareness.

Developing an accurate assessment of the team's strengths, competencies, and challenges

According to Goleman and others who define emotional intelligence, we are more likely to be smart about our emotions when we know ourselves enough to understand accurately our strengths and challenges (a.k.a. weaknesses). The same is true for teams: A group's identity is derived largely from its core competencies and skills. A group can develop confidence in itself based on a growing and pervasive sense that it does well what it was formed to do. But this has to be an accurate assessment; it must be based on reality. For teams, a sense of their real strengths and their real challenges are formed from internal perceptions strengthened by external information and feedback. The key to expanding team self-awareness, then, is the team's ability to gather and integrate as much genuine, unbiased, reality-based internal and external information about itself as it can, and to review this information periodically.

How does the team do this? Here are five useful strategies that a team can employ to build a more accurate self-assessment.

1. **Measure performance against preset standards, and analyze this quality data.**

    Effective teams integrate their operations with accepted quality management systems, which require a team to assess and define (in advance) satisfactory and excellent performance, and, by inference, sub-standard performance. When an objective, easily measured performance standard that has a high degree of relevance to what the team does as a group can be set, the team benefits from subsequent information about how well it met this standard. Quality measurement provides credible feedback about team performance. Indeed, effective teams want their performance measured, as long as the measurements are valid and the performance standards are meaningful. A team whose identity is based on a commitment to exceeding performance standards needs information about whether this identity is based in reality. Quality measurement provides this reality check.

2. **Conduct regular customer surveys.**

   Project teams need regular and meaningful feedback from their customers. Surveys should be built around the CHEEARS model of meta-level client relationship management described earlier. They should elicit client or stakeholder opinions about the team's competence (especially how well it meets client expectations), integrity, level of understanding of the client's challenges, ease of interaction and doing business, ability to follow up on client-raised issues, accessibility and responsiveness, and efficacy of sharing valuable and relevant information.

   Other aspects of a periodic survey can be specific to a recent project task or mini-project: Customers can provide timely and immediate feedback about recent team behaviors focused on client-desired outcomes. Teams need to dedicate time to reviewing the survey results, and to seeking additional information when any feedback is not clear. Further, teams need to act on feedback that exposes weaknesses in the team's performance. Doing so has the doubly positive effect of improving the weak area and demonstrating to the client that the feedback it provided was meaningful, and contributed to positive changes.

3. **Recognize team excellence.**

Effective teams know what excellent performance is. This point was covered earlier when we described establishing performance standards against which the team's performance is measured. But effective teams do more than simply understand when excellent performance occurs—they acknowledge and celebrate these instances. Awards, team recognition events, or other acknowledgements of team performance excellence are most meaningful when they correspond to team values. Examples of this type of self-awareness-promoting behavior might be "Caught Providing Superior Customer Service" awards, recognition for the best and most provocative new suggestion brought up in a team idea-generating session, or pizza luncheons for meeting a project milestone ahead of schedule. These types of values-congruent acts of recognition are a great way to build team morale and reinforce the affirmative environment the group needs to maintain. Teams and project leaders can establish these awards at early stages of the team's formation or throughout the team's life. They are part self-awareness enhancers, and part shared team value reinforcement strategies.

Incidents that vividly portray that the team is performing in accordance with its beliefs and values should be communicated within the team. If an award system is not used, then the "good news" should be disseminated by e-mail, by acknowledgement at team meetings, or both. Large measurable successes, such as having the project renewed by the client, receiving a performance bonus from the client for exceeding performance standards, or other victories may warrant a company-sponsored party or celebration. This may range from providing lunch at a team meeting (food is a great reward for most of us!) to developing an off-site celebration that members will enjoy (and maybe choose themselves). The value of strategies to recognize team performance is more than the feel-good morale boost it provides. Team recognition reinforces team values that are critical to the group's self-awareness.

4. **Review Lessons Learned.**

    Effective teams pause to reflect on how they performed in pursuit of a goal or milestone, after the milestone has been reached. The reality is that often teams are under such tight performance deadlines and expectations that this reflection is best saved for a time after the heat is off and members have more perspective on how the team conducted its work. "Lessons Learned" reviews are self-critical processes that help teams consider performance-related and process-related information that is apparent to members of the group, but has not been synthesized as yet. It is a process of internal feedback from the team to the team. Although it is a self-critical exercise, the tone of this session needs to remain positive. The focus of this effort is on future improvement in processes that can achieve better results. Lessons Learned sessions require the members to demonstrate emotional intelligence, to understand that the point of having these meetings is team learning and team self-understanding, rather than individual performance evaluations. The attitudes of members during this process need to be nondefensive and self-examining, with an acceptance that team effectiveness is based on an accurate assessment of what it does well...and not so well. It is a unique opportunity to frame all assessments—positive and negative—in terms of the team, thus reinforcing team identity and the relationships of members to the team itself.

Hint! Use lateral thinking processes for Lessons Learned reviews. See Habit #5 for an explanation of this habit of highly effective teams.

5. Retreat

Along the same vein—of the value of reflection away from the stressors of day-to-day project performance—effective teams understand that there is a great deal of value in conducting intermittent retreats that bring members together in a external context to review team values, goals, norms, processes, and any other aspect of team self-awareness that benefits from intermittent review. Some retreats are focused on planning for the future, but even these types of retreats benefit from exercises that reinforce team identity. The future is largely contingent on what exists today.

Why does the team need to get away to take part in these types of reflective exercises? The answer is partly practical and partly dynamic. The practical aspect is that it removes people from their immediate responsibilities and allows them to focus on process issues on a broader scale without interruption. The dynamic issue is one of "granting permission" to be reflective and to *process* and *synthesize* information, rather than acting on it. Members often feel that reflection is a luxury of time that they cannot afford—not with clients breathing down their necks with high expectations. But taking time for reflection is an important behavior of leaders and successful people, and retreats reinforce this by creating an environment and setting a tone whereby the team can focus on and expand their reflective self-awareness comfortably.

Formal team self-evaluations

Research within organizations, as presented by Elizabeth Stubbs, demonstrates that high-performing teams are much likelier than average teams to engage in self-diagnosis and monitor their own performance. This self-evaluation addresses both interpersonal climate and tangible output. We concur from our empirical observations of effective teams—they periodically take time to conduct self-surveys about their strengths and weaknesses. Measuring team effectiveness provides a "score," typically reflecting a composite average of all measures in the survey. Based on whatever type of rating scale is used, this score benchmarks the team's self-analysis of performance. Then subsequent surveys' scores can be used for comparison against previous findings. Teams can use self-assessment instruments to self-evaluate important aspects of team identity, or they can develop their own surveys. In Appendix A, we provide a sample self-evaluation instrument that any team can self-administer at any time. It has 36 dimensions of team effectiveness, based on the 6 Habits of Highly Effective Teams model and its skill-building suggestions. A scoring methodology is described as well.

Some teams may choose not to perform a formal survey, but instead to hold project team meetings periodically, during which an agenda is followed that is entirely devoted to team self-evaluation. Team leaders review mission statements and team norms, and pose questions for discussion around these aspects of team identity. After reviewing the definition of team emotional intelligence (being self-aware, adaptable and flexible, caring and empathetic, and competent in managing external relationships), teams can discuss examples of emotionally intelligent and less-than emotionally intelligent behavior in the group. As with project-specific Lessons Learned sessions, the emphasis for this discussion is always on the team itself and team behaviors. This type of review reinforces the distinct team identity that effective teams seek. Personal reflections on one's own behavior are encouraged, but always in the context of trying to improve overall team self-awareness. This session must never resort to blaming others in the group or attacking them for team-diminishing behaviors. Some teams ban the use of the word *you* or names in these sessions: Participants must use either *I* or *we* or *the team*. An accurate team self-assessment is always the purpose of this discussion— it is never focused on any particular member's shortcomings. This norm needs to be stated explicitly in advance, and maintained by the team whenever this type of self-evaluation occurs.

Providing the team with a means to improve its emotional literacy

One of the attributes of an individual with emotional intelligence is **emotional self-awareness**. The same is true for a team. An effective team knows what feelings it is experiencing, and is able to label them correctly. This skill is referred to as "emotional literacy"—being able to attribute the correct emotional label to a specific feeling. Individual emotional literacy among team members can raise the overall emotional literacy of the group, as people hear emotional labels and connect them to the shared feeling they perceive. Teams that are highly dedicated to the concept of building team emotional intelligence can distribute lists of emotional words to members, or post them in common areas. This list that promotes the team's emotional literacy should be broad and inclusive in emotional scope, and reflect the different gradients of emotions, such as the difference between *pleased* or *glad* and *elated*. When members see this list in the team's workspace, it reinforces the importance of using the best emotional word for the emotion that is being felt or worked through.

Summary

Why is team self-awareness important? Because it builds a team's emotional capacity and confidence. It is a process not unlike expanding individual self-awareness. When teams clarify their values, pursue an accurate self-assessment, and improve emotional literacy, they enhance their self-awareness.

Team behaviors that expand self-awareness of the team entity itself include:

▶ Naming the team.

▶ Developing a mission statement.

▶ Developing a team credo, its "we believe..." statements.

▶ Integrating with the organization's quality measurement systems to analyze relevant data that accurately reflects the team's performance.

▶ Recognizing excellence within the team, tied to the team's expressed values.

▶ Conducting Lessons Learned reviews after major project phases are complete.

▶ Retreating/reflecting about itself "outside the office."

▶ Completing, computing scores from, and evaluating periodic self-evaluation surveys or reviews.

▶ Distributing vocabulary words that reinforce the team's emotional literacy, and apply this literacy within team interactions.

CHAPTER 7

Habit #3:
Practicing Empathy
and Respectfulness

...Once you have been able to see the other person's point of view, your own comments will have to be drastically revised. You will find the emotion going out of the discussion, the differences being reduced, and those differences that remain being of a rational and understandable sort. —Carl Rogers, in *On Becoming a Person*

As Steven Covey says, highly effective people seek first to understand. They are empathetic, which means they prioritize understanding over imposing one's own views on others. This is a cornerstone skill for emotionally intelligent, socially adept people. So too is this skill characteristic of highly effective groups. Groups include multiple people, with multiple sets of information and perspectives. How will groups learn what they need to know or gain perspectives from fellow team members if they are not able to promote mutual understanding? An individual on a solo assignment may get away with self-centered thinking and behaviors, but a team cannot: It must be other-oriented, by the very nature of its purpose and composition. Teams exist to foster sharing, cooperation, and work coordination with others. These intrinsic factors of teams will not emerge if members make no effort to understand what others wish to contribute to the group effort.

Seeking first to understand is a relationship-building skill. Because teams need to develop three sets of interconnected relationships, this effort to understand must be directed toward each other, toward the team itself, and toward clients being served. Empathy demonstrates caring, and relationships are built upon caring behaviors. Put differently, we all want to be cared for—it goes to the very heart of human nature and to the development of close interpersonal bonds.

We reviewed the essence of empathy in *6 Habits of Highly Effective Bosses*, defining it as "the capacity to understand and respond effectively to the unique circumstances of another." One of the other six habits of supervisory leadership we espouse is applying Golden Rule Principles—treating others the way we would want to be treated by *our* boss, putting ourselves in others' positions to gain perspective about how they feel in certain circumstances. It occurs to us that this Golden Rule habit is really an extension of self-awareness and practicing empathy. We treat others as we wish to be treated when we make an effort to understand who they are and how they are feeling. From this other-oriented empathetic effort, we can combine this understanding of them with our emotionally self-aware reaction to the same situation, and develop a course of action that aligns these two understandings in keeping with our core values and beliefs.

The primary behavioral manifestation of applying Golden Rule Principles that we noted in *6 Habits of Highly Effective Bosses* was showing respect. Respectfulness is empathetic behavior—it is other-oriented, it prioritizes understanding, and it demonstrates caring and an ability to read situations and people. Everyone wants to be treated with respect; it is fundamental to our sense of self-esteem, to our sense that we matter to others. And certainly, it is essential to relationship-building. Nothing kills a relationship faster than a lack of respect. This is true when the lack of respect is directed toward another team member, toward the team itself, or certainly toward another team in the organization or to a team's customers.

Due to the extent to which they share so many intrinsic aspects, empathy and respectfulness are combined into a single habit characteristic of effective teams. We believe they are woven from the same fabric of interpersonal caring.

Let's review once again the essence of interpersonal empathy and effective empathetic behavior in organizations. This skill's essential characteristics include:

▸ Seeking first to understand.

▸ Being other-oriented.

▸ Feeling "with" the other person or other people.

▸ Listening actively.

▸ Practicing empathetic interpersonal methods: slowing down, noting one's own physical reactions, applying one's own relevant past history to the other person or people (without reverting to self-orientation), setting limits on extraneous, tangential content, and focusing on the affective (emotional) reality.

We believe team members can learn to be more empathetic. It is true that some of us bring a more empathetic core to our team experiences, but the fact is that empathy is a skill that can be developed. The starting point for increasing team and team member empathy is simple recognition of what empathy is, and why it is such an important skill to develop for those on a team who share a common purpose. Teams must understand that team empathy drives team relationships, which then drive team effectiveness. Therefore, team behavioral norms need to be built around the prospect of maximizing team empathy. The shared behavioral standards of the group must place the highest priority on understanding, on listening, and not on an individual team members' self-centered orientation. Once team members "get" this—that teamwork is an other-oriented phenomenon—they are well on their way to building an environment that fosters all the other habits of highly effective teams.

Secondly, empathetic teams listen empathetically. Some refer to this behavior as "active listening," but the "active" part of this description is really just pointing out that the listener is: (1) engaged in the interaction, and (2) engaged with an attitude of external orientation rather than self-orientation. We become active listeners when our listening is not focused on ourselves, on our own needs and unique perspectives.

Indeed, the essence of *poor* listening is self-orientation. The characteristics of poor listening (that lack empathy) include:

Listening

Poor

▶ Spending time rehearsing what to say in the midst of trying to listen to what others are saying to us.

▶ Rushing in to the speaker's aid, with instant ideas about how to "fix" situations with one's good advice.

▶ Picking up only certain content or phrases and ignoring the rest.

▶ Making up one's mind before the speaker completes his or her attempt to share.

▶ Connecting everything a speaker shares to him or herself, ignoring the unique aspects of a situation.

Teams that listen this way to each other will never develop team empathy, because members' listening is self-oriented. Rather, team effectiveness is centered on listening that has these characteristics:

▶ A desire to be other-directed, rather than to project one's own feelings and ideas onto others.

▶ A desire to be nondefensive, rather than to protect the self. When the self is being protected, it is difficult to focus on another person.

▶ A desire to imagine the roles, perspectives, or experiences of the other, rather than assuming they are the same as one's own.

▶ A desire to listen as a receiver, not as a critic, and a desire to understand the other person rather than to achieve either agreement from or change in that person.

The skills that drive empathetic listening are listed and described in the following table, which makes use of Marisue Pickering's research at the University of Maine.

Figure 8: Empathetic Listening Skills

Active listening skills used by teams	Skill description and team examples
Attending, acknowledging, supporting	Providing verbal or nonverbal aware-ness of and support to the other team members—for example, eye contact, nodding one's head, and smiling. *Effective teams are attentive to each other, and show listening behaviors that support idea-sharing and demonstrate that attention is being paid.*
Restating, paraphrasing	Responding to a team member's basic verbal message, by restating it for others to hear. *This skill is simple, yet effective: Members begin responses to others with bridges such as, "So, let's be clear that the team understands what we just heard...." Then the content the previous speaker shared is paraphrased without modification or subjective interpretation. It may be valuable to then ask the speaker to confirm that this restated content was paraphrased accurately, so that the team can move forward with this acknowledged understanding.*

Reflecting	Reflecting feelings, experiences, or content that has been heard or perceived through various observable cues. *When a team member reflects a feeling—"It seems the team is frustrated right now"—he or she is moving the group forward with an important understanding. And at the same time, the reflected feeling fosters team self-awareness and team relationships.*
Summarizing, interpreting, synthesizing	Offering a tentative interpretation about the other's feelings, desires, or meanings. *Any interpretation of the content shared by another member of the group (as opposed to simply paraphrasing what was heard) is tentative, and effective teams understand this. They know that understanding is built when team members make an effort to synthesize prior information and develop team insights drawn from what is known thus far. Team empathy is manifested in understanding that interpretations are not the end, but a means by which teams gain broader understanding by bringing together a set of smaller understandings. Being wrong in these interpretations is more than okay, it is valuable, because the team understands that it needs something to which to react.*

Checking perceptions	Finding out if interpretations and perceptions are valid and accurate. *Empathetic teams listen and value efforts to summarize and synthesize perceptions. Then, they demonstrate the essence of empathy in showing the patience to discover, "Do we truly understand this issue and its implications?" Checking perceptions of team members is empathetic, because it reflects an understanding that interpretations are only that—a tentative "first crack" at understanding, which then needs to be reviewed before being assimilated into the team's shared knowledge. Effective teams go around the table to learn how others respond to an interpretation, to make sure that time is allotted to an inclusive process of listening to all input. Teams demonstrate empathy when they take the time to let the story unfold.*
Probing	Questioning team members, but in a supportive way that requests more information or that attempts to clear up confusion. *The key to this team listening behavior is bridging from the content that was shared to the probing question, which needs to be asked in an open-ended format: "Tell us more about what you mean by..." or, "That was valuable information. Let's review what it means in more depth. Share with us how...."*

Giving feedback	Sharing perceptions in reaction to the other's ideas or feelings, disclosed from a vantage point of adding to the information from which the group can benefit. *Effective teams use the Sandwich Technique if the feedback involves any type of constructive criticism. This is a relationship-enhancing method of communicating feedback in a way that promotes its ability to be heard and understood. "What you shared is very valuable, it adds a lot to what the team needs to know at this point. It seems, though, that there are pieces missing. Tell us more about...." Then, the team needs to support the other's answer. "That is the clarification we needed. Now the team has a better grasp on what the core problems are."*

Teams with empathetic listening skills built into their day-to-day processes make a conscious effort to:

▶ **Respond or react to what is left unspoken.**

"I am hearing a lot about [issue], but I sense all of us are sitting here right now with anxiety about how the client reacted the last time we tried to make a change like this."

▶ **Set aside biases and prejudices.**

Team empathy is expressed by nonjudgmental attitudes among members, who listen without instantly dismissing what they hear based on personal bias.

▶ **Connect with another member's emotions without getting too carried away with them.**

If team members express anger, disappointment, or even excessive optimism about a team issue, empathetic teams continue to try to understand as opposed to engaging in knee-jerk reactions to the strong emotions they are observing. Here's an example of an empathetic team response to several members' overt anger: "It seems that at least some members of the team are really angry about this decision. Let's make sure we understand why this is so." This approach is in contrast to one in which other team members "push back" in anger, based on discomfort with angry emotions being shared in the group.

▶ **Focus and concentrate on the team interaction without distraction.**

Distractions diminish the potential for empathy and team understanding. Members who get calls on their cell phones in a team meeting, and members who carry on side conversations as another member is speaking are common examples of team behaviors that diminish the opportunity for teams to listen empathetically. Team norms should address expected behaviors that promote the team's ability to focus and concentrate on what the team is considering at a given point in time.

▶ **Be comfortable with occasional silence, when it facilitates reflection or allows a team member to continue without interruption.**

Silence within a team setting can be meaningful. The most important aspect of a team's empathetic listening is to allow a team member to complete his or her thought without interruption, even when this speaker has paused. Again, empathetic listening asks, "Do we understand? Have we let the story unfold?"

The connection from these listening skills to the desired outcome of establishing an environment of team cohesion is direct and straightforward. Listening is the cornerstone of interpersonal interaction and understanding. So much of what a team does is centered on listening because it is an interpersonal process required by any interdependent group. It is a skill reinforced by establishing and maintaining team norms that pertain to how members show caring and respect for each other. Empathetic listening is respectful!

Listening is a skill that individual team members need to practice in all aspects of their lives. When effective, empathetic listening becomes part of respective members' interpersonal style, it is far easier for the team to assimilate norms built around the behaviors described previously. Empathetic listening is as much an individual skill as it is a team participation skill. It is far easier to conform to healthy team norms developed to reinforce empathetic listening if team members understand the importance of this skill and build it into their everyday lives.

Empathy and conflict within teams

Effective groups understand that conflict and emotionally uncomfortable situations are inevitable—and often useful—aspects of the group's activities. Team members will not agree on everything all the time, and if they do, that would be a problem in and of itself! Indeed, teams resonate with members when different backgrounds, skill sets, and viewpoints can be effectively integrated into a shared group effort. Effective teams challenge each other, raise "what if?" questions, explore alternatives (even unpopular ones), and welcome intrateam (as well as external) performance feedback as a way to assess whether the team is operating at its peak. All these behaviors raise the potential for conflict, but they also add value. Conflict poses the possibility that differences might have an immediate deleterious impact on team morale and make members uncomfortable, but it also demonstrates where the gaps are, and where potential team dysfunction is centered. Only through seeking first to understand the real issues within the team can the process begin in which the conflict is differentiated and resolved. Teams with empathy reinforce emotionally intelligent responses to the anger, disappointment, hurt feelings, and other emotional fallout of conflict. Again, these are emotional situations that will arise almost inevitably in a team challenged to deliver a complex project. Empathetic teams seek to understand these feelings without getting too carried away with them.

The norms for managing conflict in a team are tied to understanding that differences need to be understood before they can be resolved. This involves team empathy directed toward depersonalizing conflicts. **The tension in a team should be directed to the friction between ideas, between alternatives, between the best operational methods or standards, but not between people (in other words, other team members).** Teams are composed of people, and people have individual opinions, and these opinions will differ (indeed, they often should, to clarify what the team's choices are). Effective teams understand that members can express different points of view, but the team needs to focus on understanding the *nature* of the different positions within the team, not on the individual team members who bring them forth or promote them. Conflict raises the potential for challenges to individual egos, but effective teams demonstrate an ability to subsume personal ego and champion a team ego, a team self. The norms that teams develop about depersonalizing conflict take all the empathy and overall emotional intelligence that members and the team itself can muster. But once an empathetic "depersonalization of conflict" norm is integrated into team behaviors and sticks, the result is a team that copes with conflict well, rather than letting conflict undermine team functioning.

Case Example

Two information technology engineers working together on a project differ in opinions about the logical next course of action in solving a problem. One engineer advocates an immediate systemic overhaul, because the problem is likely to repeat itself. The time is right for such a mini-project, she insists. The other engineer advocates a short-term, work-around fix, to please the client, before any major overhaul is undertaken. In the course of this discussion, one engineer insists rather angrily, "My way will end up saving dollars in the long run." The other engineer quickly retorts, "There won't be any dollars if we don't fix this problem soon, because they will kick us out!" The discussion continues, with both engineers hardening in their respective positions. One of the two engineers finally states, "The team has to decide whether it is best to choose my plan or his." Team members move quickly to reframe the way this conflict is heading—personal. One member reminds the others that, "It is not a difference between the two of you—it is a conflict between two sensible approaches with different immediate and longer-term return on investment." Members focus the conflict on the relative merits and downsides of the two *approaches*, not on the two engineers who presented them. The subsequent discussions included reminders of the team's core values related to client satisfaction and long-term relationship building. In the end, the team found common ground, deciding on a plan that incorporated an immediate work-around fix along with establishment of a change management task group (to include client representatives) to explore more comprehensive system modifications that needed to be implemented.

Respectfulness

Empathetic listening is one important way that teams show respect for each other and for the team itself. In what other ways does the effective team demonstrate an ability to be respectful?

Honesty

Nothing interferes with teams building respect and trust for each other like dishonesty, among team members or by the team itself to its members or customers. Teams need to value the truth, no matter how much it might hurt to acknowledge it. Honest communication prevents situations in which teams pursue pathways that are not based on real issues or events. Honesty fuels mutual accountability, which goes to the very nature of what makes a team a team. When teams respect each others' viewpoints and input, that respect is based on the fundamental assumption that all communication within the team is open and completely truthful.

Team self-evaluations should include an assessment about whether the team:

▸ Tolerates and even embraces complete candor by members.

▸ Trusts each other, and how much that trust is tied to team honesty.

▸ Challenges any communications or behaviors that may be intentionally misleading.

Fairness/doing what's right

Unequal treatment of others and fundamental inequities within the team diminish an environment of mutual respect. How might inequities emerge in a team? Examples might include:

▸ **Uneven information-sharing across the team,** so that some members are privy to certain information and others are not. Teams need to instill information-sharing practices that are relatively blind to roles or positions on the team, and spread data and news across the team uniformly and equally.

▸ **Changing a team member's role without sufficient advance notice and/or without adequate rationale.** Team morale is built on understanding and executing one's role on the team in coordination with others, and morale dissipates rapidly when a team member has the rug pulled out from under him or her. Even if there is a rationale for this decision by a project team leader, it is best to allow the team input, and give them time to process the implications of the change.

> ▶ **Higher visibility to the customer or client for some members of the team, and not for others.** This is a morale-reducer when there is no business reason for such differences within the team regarding the extent of client contact members have. Effective teams are inclusive, and are uncomfortable excluding members from any meetings or interactions unless there is a clear and evident reason behind this approach.

> ▶ **Uneven distribution of more tedious or more difficult tasks.** Team members need to chip in evenly to do the more unpleasant tasks of a project, especially if there are no clear expectations about which member is best suited for the task. Conversely, when all members demonstrate their willingness to be part of chores that everyone acknowledges are tedious or tiresome, then teams build a sense of shared responsibility regardless of position or role. The age-old axiom from baseball of "taking one for the team" is borne out in this premise, that there are times to do the unpleasant things in order to promote the sense that the team is a single entity and "we are all in this together."

Case Example

A proposal development team is behind schedule, and it is clear that final production of the proposal document will need to be done in a shorter time frame than usual. The members of the team in charge of production give up their weekend to finish the process. When they arrive on Saturday morning, they are surprised to see all the leaders for the development of different sections of the proposal present, asking how they can help. With these extra sets of hands and resources, doing rather basic functions such as copying documents and preparing three-ring binders, the team is able to finish production earlier than expected, which frees up precious weekend time for the production team who had worked three of the previous four weekends as well.

Think of the team unity that such "rolling up one's sleeves and pitching in" types of behavior by senior members of the team can promote!

Embrace diversity on the team

Respecting differences on the team is an important aspect of teamwork. Differences need to be respected, not just because they are likely to occur in any team comprising different types of people with different skill sets, but also because they add value. Diverse backgrounds, perspectives, and interests provide the team with richer and more robust sources of information and performance competencies. Diverse teams can rally around common purposes and norms. But this conformance to team behavioral expectations does not preclude that diversity from manifesting itself in very positive ways. Diversities should be identified and solicited as a resource to the team. This is especially true in efforts by the team to understand the external client, customer, or stakeholder. In part, client understandings are based on optimal information about all aspects of the client and its needs. A diverse team has a greater opportunity to anticipate a client's needs, and to develop the previously discussed "currencies" that can be exchanged to fuel an effective client relationship. Indeed, the more diverse the client and the client representatives, the more diverse a team should be to understand client needs assessments.

Summary

Teams need to be other-oriented. They must seek to understand, and to care, about themselves, their teammates, and their clients/stakeholders. Empathy and showing respect are connected by the willingness to be other-oriented, to prioritize understanding over the imposition of personal viewpoints, and to demonstrate a range of caring behaviors.

Effective teams are active listeners. This means that members:

▶ Are nondefensive, rather than listening through a filter of self-protection.

▶ Accept the unique perspectives or experiences of the other members of the team, rather than assuming they are the same as their own.

▶ Listen as a receiver, not as a critic, with a desire to understand the other member rather than to achieve either agreement or change from that teammate.

Effective teams are able to exchange ideas through listening and group communication methods that demonstrate empathy. These include:

▶ Supporting and being attentive.

▶ Rephrasing content.

▶ Reflecting feelings.

▶ Summarizing, interpreting, and synthesizing.

▶ Checking perceptions with each other, and making interpretations.

▶ Probing and giving feedback.

Teams show respect in many ways, including:

▶ Being honest and valuing candor.

▶ Avoiding and/or confronting inequities, demonstrating fundamental fairness.

▶ Embracing diversity.

CHAPTER 8

Habit #4:
Establishing and Regulating
Team Norms

*[Team effectiveness] requires a team atmosphere
in which...norms build emotional capacity [the
ability to respond constructively in emotionally
uncomfortable situations] and influence behaviors in constructive ways.* —V.U. Druskatt and
S.B. Wolff

Norms are both implicit and explicit rules of behavior. Implicit norms in teams are those that are evident and understood, but not necessarily documented or spoken about. A team's explicit norms are those that the team considers, agrees to, documents or codifies, and abides by. According to Druskat and Wolff, group level norms are those that guide a group's behaviors to produce a positive emotional consequence for the group. A team uses norms as a guidepost, especially when the group goes off course. Norms are inevitable elements of group interaction—they form whether they are formally discussed or not. In the end, establishing and maintaining healthy group norms has a very profound positive effect on a team's functional capabilities.

Team norming is a process driven by both personal and social factors. Individuals have needs and interests, but one of these needs is to belong; we attribute part of our identity to the groups to which we invest emotional energy. Members' behavior creates a team social culture, encompassing beliefs, customs, knowledge, and practices. Members depend on the team culture to give the group stability, security, understanding, and the ability to respond to a given situation.

The chart on the following page illustrates this concept.

Figure 9: Impact of Relative Individualization and Socialization on a Team

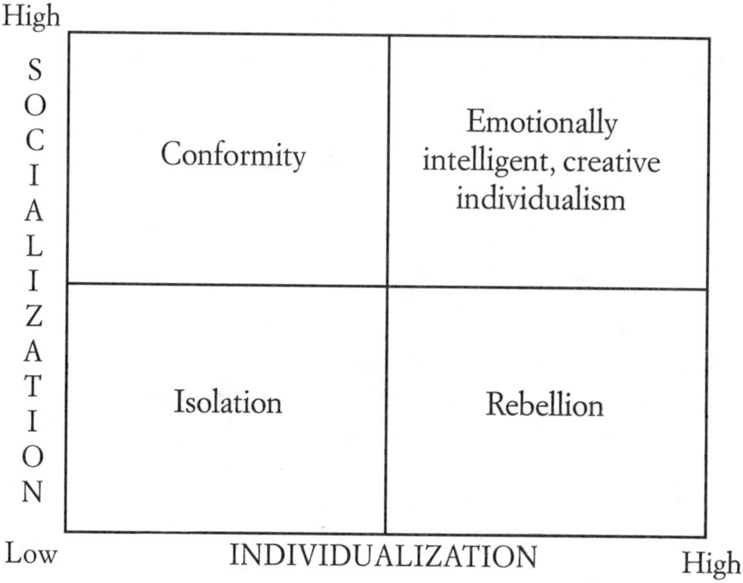

High

S O C I A L I Z A T I O N	Conformity	Emotionally intelligent, creative individualism
	Isolation	Rebellion

Low   INDIVIDUALIZATION   High

This chart shows the ways relative individualization and socialization efforts affect different teams:

▶ Low socialization and low individualization creates member isolation within the team.

▶ Low socialization and high individualization creates member rebellion against the team.

▶ High socialization and low individualization creates conformity. The individual is subsumed within the team—"there is no 'I' in team"—with deference to the team and its culture. If the team's social values reflect one's own, then conformity is a values-congruent norming process. If they don't, then it is a more passive form of conformity.

▶ High socialization and high individualization help foster a creative environment. The individualization, however, needs to be emotionally intelligent. It needs to see the value of both self-awareness and self-management, *and* social awareness and social management.

In essence, this "creativity" quadrant where high individualization and high socialization exist is populated by those emotionally intelligent enough to see that teams require social rules, but at the same time can promote expressions of individuality that add to the team's perspectives. This process may require a balancing act. Individualism favors individual rights, loosely knit social networks, self-respect, and personal rewards and careers—all of which are good things in and of themselves. Socialization or collectivism favors the group, builds harmony, and asks, "What is best for the group, or the organization?" This too is good. Teams thrive when their members can find a way in their norming process to establish standards that promote shared values, while allowing members to express creative, group-enhancing aspects of their individual self. The norming challenge for teams is to promote creativity while still maintaining the culture that binds the group into a purposeful social system.

There is a bit of a "chicken and egg" dynamic at work in describing the value of establishing and enforcing team norms. Do norms come first, and drive a team's emotionally intelligent behaviors? Or are the norms an extension of the team's essential values and skills relevant to emotionally intelligent behaviors? The answer, in most cases, is that both sequences occur. And it really doesn't matter! Either way, teams need to demonstrate emotional capacity, manage their relationships, expand self-awareness, and practice empathy. It may be that the norms provide a model for empathetic behavior, causing members with less native emotional intelligence to become more and more comfortable expressing these behaviors as a result of observing and mirroring them. In other instances, norming simply validates the effective team behaviors that members possess already, and therefore bring to the team.

From a team leadership perspective, Tuckerman's group development model anticipates that norms, even if formulated from the very outset, will be tested. That is okay. It is far better to have established norms to draw this testing behavior than to drift into team projects without any clear set of behavioral guidelines that reflect the team's values. Our experience is that time dedicated to norm development at the earliest stages of project team formation, within a meeting that is well-led and inclusive of team representatives, is a model starting point for any project team. Once the team understands why it has formed and what its purposes and objectives are, the next logical focus of team attention is on the process of "how we are going to get there." And the team's process effectiveness is highly contingent on how well it develops, integrates, and is guided by the norms it establishes to determine how it will go about achieving its purposes.

Implicit norms generally reflect expected interpersonal behaviors within the team that build or reinforce the team's overall emotional intelligence. It is impossible to codify and document every single behavior for every potential group circumstance. Norms that are unstated but well integrated into the emotional fabric of an effective team are best understood by asking the question, "Is this the way every team member expects the others to behave? Is this the way we as a team and every individual member within this team would want to be treated?" Implicit norms apply Golden Rule Principles, discussed in Habit #3, practicing empathy and respectfulness.

Revisiting norms

Project teams evolve as they perform their tasks throughout the project lifecycle. The people on the project may change, or task leadership may move from one individual to another, based on project planning and which sequential milestone is approaching. Technical processes are very likely to change throughout a team-based project, or at the very least be improved upon as corrective action is taken stemming from periodic quality reviews. In this environment of adapting to project changes, teams need to revisit their norms periodically. At the very least, such an action by the team simply reinforces the norms to which members adhere. It provides a type of "regrounding" or "refresher training" about a critical aspect of team effectiveness. Additionally, it bolsters a team's self-awareness (Habit #2). Periodic reviews and updates about a team's norms provide an opportunity for the team to get back in touch with its core values and shared behavioral expectations. Obviously, this review is essential when the team leader, or any member, believes norms are being routinely ignored, sidestepped, or violated in any way. Similar to a computer game with a reset button that reverts the game back to its baseline operation, a review of team norms can get all team members back on the same page.

Establishing and periodically reviewing team norms has an additional value-adding component—these team development activities reinforce the consequences that apply when team norms are ignored or violated. Most often, the consequences of behavior outside of team norms is simply that the norm-offending team member will receive input from others on the team that, "This is not how our team does things," or, "This is not how we agreed to do things." Usually, this type of feedback is sufficient to steer the member who is "off the reservation" back into the fold. But teams need to consider and share an understanding—either implicit or explicit—about what the consequences will be for persistent, and seemingly intentional, violations of team norms. Obviously, the ultimate "capital punishment" consequence is removal of the team member in favor of one who can abide by team norms. For those of us who participated in any type of team sport, there was always a clear understanding about the consequences of non-adherence to team rules—if you don't conform to them, you don't play. It's as simple as that. Some team leaders and teams express and document this consequence overtly. Others simply demonstrate it with their reactions to a member's nonconforming behavior—they are taken off the field by the leader, with the support of the team members. Team members are far more likely to be benched if they do not follow the team's norms than if they do not perform as skillfully as the team would like. Skills can be practiced and refined. Coaching can draw out skills that may be latent or lacking, but deliberate behaviors that undermine the team's processes and methods are emotionally hostile, and must be confronted, by the team and its leader acting as a cohesive unit.

The team norming process

Highly effective teams convene a meeting to generate their norms. At the earliest possible stage of a team's project life cycle, the issue of norming requires conscious deliberation. This process is a project management requirement—discussions of work plans and assignments should proceed after discussions of team norms and behavioral guidelines.

Team norming is an inclusive process. Inclusiveness reduces the Forming and Storming resistance that Tuckerman's model anticipates. It is important that the values of the team reflect the values of both the members and team leader. An initial consideration for any team that forms is the types of behaviors that are important to team members and by which they intend to abide. This discussion elicits agreements on basic processes and approaches to the project work, and to behaviors that foster teamwork.

The following are some examples of issues to discuss during this norming session:

▶ How will the team come to closure about an agenda item? How will the team make decisions? Will the majority rule? Or should the team achieve consensus to implement a decision? Or is the team in essence a consultant to a leader who has ultimate decision-making responsibility?

▶ What team behaviors promote project time management and time efficiencies? What will the team's expectations be about meeting attendance, promptness, preparedness, documentation, and dissemination of team proceedings?

▶ How will meeting agendas be set?

▶ How will the team work through an issue? Whose viewpoints matter? What is a member's responsibility to contribute to the discussion of an outstanding issue?

▶ How will team members be accountable to one another?

▶ What behaviors are encouraged or expected, and which behaviors will not be tolerated or should be confronted by the team when they occur because they add no value to—or even detract from—the team's work? In particular, teams need to consider and create normative expectations about team courtesy: listening to each other, seeking first to understand, and not interrupting each other in discussions.

▶ What behaviors reinforce an affirmative environment in the team? How does the group regulate its need to remain positive and optimistic?

▶ How will the team handle conflict and differences of opinion? Also, it needs to have an understanding of what behavior differentiates healthy assertiveness from behavior that is born out of destructive anger and unwillingness to seek common ground.

▶ How will project plan changes be approved and implemented?

▶ Who interacts directly with the customer(s), client(s), and stakeholders? Is there a Single Point of Contact methodology, or is the team empowered to communicate with client peers (based on its understanding of the client's wishes or preferences)? What behaviors around or with customers are expected, and which are verboten?

▶ How will client complaints be prioritized and handled?

▶ How will information be gathered and disseminated? Who needs to be on which e-mail distribution list, tied to which functions?

▶ How will conference calls be led? What behaviors are expected on these conference calls in order to optimize participation and valuable input from call participants; optimize peoples' productivity and the time dedicated to these conference calls by the entire group; facilitate discussions; share valuable information; and move through the agenda expediently.

These are ideas about norms that effective teams consider. It is not an all-inclusive list, by any means. The team needs to determine how granular they wish to get in establishing these norms. Yet the previously cited issues provide a useful framework for developing norms that reinforce productivity, teamwork, and the emotional capacity to manage uncomfortable situations. They help a team remain proactive, and maintain an affirmative environment within the team.

Leading this norming session requires a balancing act, involving the need to promote shared values driving the norms and the need for the leader to outline his or her project management methodology. In most instances, team members' norms coalesce around the same norms that the team leader wishes to promulgate. In the rare circumstance when this does not happen, and a unilateral norm is, in essence, ordered by the team leader, the rationale for the norm needs to be explained thoroughly. The team leader should anticipate that any norms that are not fully embraced by the team are those that are likely to draw resistant behaviors from members.

When should norming occur? It needs to occur early, but is there a recommended sequence within which the norming process should be inserted? New project teams tend to begin with explanations/sharing of team identity ("who we are"), purpose ("why we are here"), challenges ("what's to be done"), and process ("how we are going to do it as a team"). Why not put the "how" before the "what"? Consider the slightly different priorities and team culture that can develop by the following two slightly different team orientation sequences:

Team 1 Orientation Sequence

1. The team leader introduces him- or herself.

2. The leader asks the team members to introduce themselves, their position, their role on the team (if they know it in advance), and what department or company they work for (in the case of a multi-organization project team).

3. The leader explains the team's purpose.

4. The leader asks for a discussion about the team's norms, which may begin with a request for members to reflect about teams they have been on that worked exceptionally well together and were extremely effective. After allowing time for this reflection, the leader reviews several norms that he or she has found very useful in effective teams. Then members are asked to contribute their experiences and suggestions for the current team. This process should yield a preliminary set of norms to which team members agree. The leader notes that these shared behavioral expectations will be written and distributed at the next meeting, and reviewed periodically.

5. The leader then begins sharing about the components of the project, project plan, deliverables, and respective team assignments.

Team 2 Orientation Sequence

Repeat steps 1, 2, and 3, but reverse steps 4 and 5.

Which process feels better to you? By norming immediately after sharing the team's purpose, the leader is connecting team process with team objectives, in a direct, sequential way.

The implication is that the team norms are paramount in the leader's mind, and crucial to the team's success. It makes a statement that the cohesiveness and mutual understandings of team process are the factors that drive the project team's ability to achieve its purpose. In instances when many divisions or separate companies come together on a project, this approach helps create a "single-badged" mentality; that is, a team in which divisional or company differences are left out of the team process, and rather, a unified team is setting its own rules to create a cohesive whole.

When norms are documented for all team members to have as a guideline for expected team behaviors, it is best to keep the list relatively short. Lists documenting team norms that are too long seem pedantic and controlling, and thereby lose their intended emotional impact. Plus, long lists are just too much for members to absorb and integrate. In general, we recommend that teams create team norms that are broad-based about the more emotional behaviors expected of team members, and be relatively specific about team norms tied to mutual accountability.

The following mock list of team norms reflects this approach.

Project Shake and Bake
Team Norms, Behaviors, and Shared Expectations

▶ All project meetings have agendas, they start and end on time, and participation is required.

▶ We listen to others in all team processes, and we respect alternative viewpoints.

▶ We do not personalize conflicts.

▶ All customer communication is channeled through the program manager.

▶ Customer complaints, preferences, and customer-relevant service quality issues have the highest level of priority for this team.

▶ E-mail distribution lists are inclusive. If you wish to be taken off a distribution list, contact the originator of the e-mail message.

▶ Project risks need to be identified (not ignored), and risk identification needs to occur as early as possible.

▶ Our team behaviors must reflect the trust we need to have in each other.

▶ Team norms will be reviewed and updated periodically.

▶ Project management decisions are the responsibility of the program manager. However, team input about all aspects of project planning and execution is both expected and valued.

▶ Team assignments are made in accordance with the "best athlete" principle: The individual or subcontractor who brings the most relevant skills to the assignment is the first choice to perform it.

▶ Communication within the team—formal and informal—is always valued. When in doubt about the value of contacting a team member, a group, or the overall team about a piece of information or communication, just do it!

There is a final norm that can be particularly useful as a way of enriching the information from which a team processes decisions. It serves to introduce the concepts that will be reviewed in the following chapter describing Habit #5, thinking laterally.

▶ We will not judge each other when we share new ideas. We encourage provocative thinking that spurs innovation.

Summary

Teams need to establish their norms, knowing that many norms are implicit and that long, granular lists of team norms are infantilizing and counter-productive. Norms should reflect team values and prior experience in particularly effective groups to which members have belonged. The focus of team norming needs to be on specific team-conforming behaviors that promote time management and communication, as well as emotionally competent group norms focused on managing team relationships. Norming occurs at an early stage of the team's meeting, which establishes shared methods and standards as preeminent in the project leader's team-building methodology. This focus on Norming also helps mitigate the Forming and Storming resistance characteristics of new teams.

CHAPTER 9

Habit #5:
Thinking Laterally

If you want to try to understand something, try to change it. —Kurt Lewin

There are many different types of projects that teams perform. Some are rather straightforward, task-oriented projects requiring redundant operations and repetitive systems. In such cases, tasks have been performed in the past, and, with a little tinkering, they will be done the same way in the immediate future. This type of project team easily understands its purpose, its performance objectives, and the approach that will be used to meet those objectives. Well-established (and sometimes long-standing) best practices are employed, and the project will be managed as other recent similar projects were managed that yielded successful outcomes. After all, solutions that work tend to be—and should be—repeated.

However, in other projects, there is more of a "green field" opportunity. Clients, or organizations themselves, have a need for innovation. They are looking for far more than simple bodies with requisite skills to handle tasks that keep the operation running smoothly. They seek a team that can assess a problem, break new ground, and create a competitive edge. Tried-and-true approaches just won't cut it. Innovation is the "value add" in many projects in which the focus is more on the future than keeping things going as they are in the present.

In instances when the objectives that drive a team's creation are tied to creativity and innovation, teams offer enormous value—or at least the potential for enormous value. Teams bring multiple skill sets, experiences, academic backgrounds, and simply more aggregate brainpower to solution-finding. Highly effective teams are able to harness the thinking assets they possess, and get these assets working together creatively and synergistically. Superior teams champion and sustain group processes that offer the opportunity to generate more ideas and new solutions.

Unfortunately, many teams are led with more straightforward approaches characterized by a team leader asking members, "Here is our dilemma—does anyone have any ideas?" Such an approach can actually detract from the goal of considering new ideas and developing new insights. When a group is asked to consider a new way of doing something, often a range of different viewpoints emerge. They vie competitively for the attention and approval of both the group leader and other members. The ascendancy of one idea over another can be a process of willpower as much as the power or value of a particular idea. The individual team member with the strongest ego, the highest standing, or the best skills in persuasion may end up dominating the idea-generating process. In the meantime, many other good and useful ideas are either never considered adequately, or are pushed aside too quickly. The process is often a contest of sorts, with many interpersonal dynamics at play that impede rather than accelerate the generation of innovative solutions.

Group synergies don't just happen—they require an approach such that people and their collective brainpower work together with others in a way that jumps the process ahead and sidesteps the struggles that weigh a group down in inertia. An intrinsic aspect of innovation and creativity is thinking differently about the same problem. It requires a group norm in which provocative thoughts are not just tolerated, but expected. And then the group needs a system to turn provocative perspectives about a particular problem or challenge into a new pattern of thinking that allows incremental jumps away from old patterns of thinking. Team synergies, which are really the Holy Grail of teamwork focused on innovation, are all about these leaps ahead in which fresh perspectives are gathered, considered, formulated, tested, and ultimately implemented.

Tolerating provocative thoughts in the context of team-based innovation requires emotional intelligence—both from individual team members and the team itself. The team needs to demonstrate the emotional capacity to tolerate ideas that, by their very provocative nature, push emotional buttons in individual members. Advancing the team environment where innovation can occur requires both individual and team emotional competencies (which are outlined in Goleman's EI model as well):

▶ **Emotional self-awareness.** Effective teams and their members need to be aware that change is an emotional process with exciting rewards if pursued skillfully. With this awareness, feelings about new ideas can be labeled and understood. For example, uncomfortable emotions attached to change, once labeled and understood by the emotionally intelligent team, can be mitigated because they are attributed to participating in a process of innovation.

▶ **Self-management competencies around flexibility, adaptability, and optimism.** By bringing these emotional competencies to teamwork focused on discovering new solutions, the effective team can avoid rigid stances and understand that emotional allegiance to what has worked before, to methods to which it is most accustomed, can be counterproductive.

▶ **Reading situations well, and showing empathy for members who "think outside the box" a bit.** Often, one's natural reaction to a provocative idea is to think instantly of why it will not work. *The high-EI team seeks first to understand*, and this attitude tolerates both the expression of different ideas, and the unbiased pursuit of the logical implications and ramifications of notions that go against traditional thinking about a problem.

▶ **Managing relationships in the team by rewarding provocative ideas,** and by forsaking an inclination to employ persuasion and influence skills when these might interfere with the process of fully exploring new ideas.

Dr. Edward de Bono has published many works on the value of what he refers to as "lateral thinking." In essence, de Bono advocates that teams charged with generating innovative solutions think in a different way—laterally, instead of the more analytical and sequential process of vertical thinking. Lateral thinking is both an attitude and a method of using information. Whereas vertical thinking is selective, lateral thinking is generative.

Dr. de Bono considers the practice of lateral thinking as a "gift," because it does not come naturally to most of us. Our view is different: We see the exercise of lateral thinking not as foreordained gift, but one that can be learned, exercised, and deployed regardless of one's natural tendencies to think more traditionally, or vertically. The training needed is as much about individual and team emotional intelligence skills as it is about the actual process of lateral thinking. Lateral thinking requires teams to be smart about their emotions. It is by no means synonymous with emotional intelligence; rather, lateral thinking is potentiated by the application of emotional intelligence skills.

According to de Bono, "lateral thinking is closely related to insight, creativity, and humor," and it is a "deliberate process." If this is so, teams charged with innovation need to take notice of the possible advantages of lateral thinking, not just because it offers the potential for innovation (derived from greater insights and creativity), but because it is brought about through a documented process. Teams are defined by their common approach, and lateral thinking approaches offer a process to help teams meet their solution-finding objectives.

Lateral thinking is a method for insight and creativity because it changes the rules about ways to deal with the conflict inherent to the process of changing one's ideas about things. As de Bono says in *Lateral Thinking*:

> Culture is concerned with establishing ideas...[and] improving them by bringing them up to date....[The] method for changing ideas is conflict, which works in two ways. In the first way there is a head-on confrontation between opposing ideas. One or the other achieves a practical dominance over the other idea, which is suppressed....In the second way, there is a conflict between new information and the old idea. As a result of this conflict the old idea is supposed to be changed....The conflict method for changing ideas works well where the information can be evaluated in some objective manner. But the method does not work well when the new information can only be evaluated through the old idea. Instead of being changed the old idea is strengthened and made even more rigid.

Consequently, Dr. de Bono insists that the most effective way of changing ideas, of finding truly innovative new solutions, is not from a conflict resolution process among the team, but from "insight rearrangement of available information." This offers the best potential for huge leaps forward. "When ideas lead information rather than lag behind," Dr. de Bono notes, "progress is rapid."

How does a team advocate for the preeminence of ideas over information, of creativity over comfort with the status quo? The process involves this notion that Dr. de Bono labels lateral thinking. New insights, de Bono notes, involve the restructuring of patterns. Creativity also involves restructuring, "but with more emphasis on the escape from restricting patterns." Lateral thinking, de Bono says:

...involves restructuring, escape, and the provocation of new patterns....Lateral thinking is concerned with the generation of new ideas. This leads to changes in attitude and approach; to looking in a different way at things which have always been looked at in the same way. Liberation from old ideas and the stimulation of new ones are twin aspects of lateral thinking.

What exactly is lateral thinking, and how does it apply specifically to effective teamwork? How do teams develop the capability to think laterally when charged with the advancement of new ideas? The basic premise of lateral thinking in teams is that members forsake the conflict method that Dr. de Bono explains is so limiting and so focused on old patterns and struggles about which idea will dominate. Rather, it requires a group norm that encourages members to think together in a similar way, laterally, as if rowing in the same direction. This type of thinking is intrinsically provocative; it engenders ideas that shake clear of old thinking patterns.

Dr. de Bono conceived a practical method for teams to practice thinking laterally. The method employs the tangible, observable symbol of a colored hat to represent six different thinking patterns that gather perspectives on an issue, problem, or challenge. It focuses team members on avoiding being locked into extremely counterproductive, emotionally driven attitudes about ideas and solutions. The lateral thinking process is part emotional regulator, and part practice in a very important team function: thinking through a problem.

Let's review Dr. de Bono's "six hats" of lateral thinking, and the thinking-related focus of each.

The **White Hat** is concerned with fact-finding thinking. This is where the team forsakes any judgments whatsoever, and concentrates only on the facts, on available information, and what the team knows and needs to know. Opinions about the information are not allowed. Team members think simply about what is known and needs to be known. This might seem a bit limiting at first, but it is amazing how much more new information comes out in a White Hat stage than it does when teams combine the process of uncovering available information with the process of judging the usefulness or applicability of that information. Part of it is simply the time factor. Time is always limited in teams, and teams' first inclination is to cut to the chase and judge the usefulness of certain information. But if the team is thinking laterally only about what it knows, the yield from White Hat-generated facts or information-gathering is far greater. Some information that might be viewed as peripheral and not worthy of consideration comes out, and ends up playing a role in an innovative solution. All relevant information (without much judgment about whether it is highly relevant or not) is encouraged when a team performs White Hat thinking.

The **Red Hat** clarifies emotional reactions to issues, team functions, team processes, and team decisions. When teams consider their emotional reactions to an issue, they are reinforcing the value of emotional self-awareness and the notion that the team as a whole has emotions and emotional intelligence. Intuitive reactions are elicited, advocated, even championed. Practical aspects of an issue are not allowed. Hunches or gut feelings play a role in teamwork and a team's decision-making, so the Red Hat gets these emotional reactions out on the table. The emotional reactions to a course of action don't tell everything about an option's potential effectiveness, but they are important aspects of decision-making. Sometimes, the best course is to follow gut reactions, which Red Hat thinking elicits. Emotions about new ideas are natural, and they must be understood.

Black Hat thinking considers the downside of an idea. There is value in seeing why an idea will not work—not as a way to kill the idea, but as a way to give it shared space in the team's decision-making process. The key to Black Hat thinking is that it not dominate and overrule any other thinking, and that it be undertaken *only* when all the members have the Black Hat on. The attitude that effective teams take is that there are always reasons not to do something, but these reasons need not overwhelm us either because of our low emotional tolerance for risk or our unilateral devotion to old patterns. By giving Black Hat negative thinking equal but not greater weight than other types of thinking, risk assessments become more even-handed.

The **Yellow Hat** is the opposite of the Black Hat. This is positive thinking, in which you concentrate on the benefits and show the sunny, optimistic side of your thinking. When groups think laterally about all the reasons why an idea is a good one, all the benefits of a new approach are elicited without fear of being shot down as unrealistic, naïve, or overshadowed by the downside. These should include the benefits to the customer. Effective teams allow themselves to tap into the emotionally intelligent competency of optimism. Often, this Yellow Hat exercise brings out new benefits with considerable value, which can counter more negativistic or pessimistic thinking elicited by the Black Hat.

Yellow goes hand-in-hand with green—creativity. The **Green Hat** is worn to develop creative ideas. All ideas are welcome. Again, no judgments are allowed. Provocative ideas are not only welcome, but expected. This is the hat that liberates a team, by bringing out all the innovativeness it has in its fiber, producing ideas that one would not have considered oneself. Although logic and organization are required to develop creative excellence, this depends on free thought. Green

Hat thinking by a team is a process whereby embryonic ideas are brought out before they can be fully hatched. When a project involves a "green field" opportunity, thinking must occur with the Green Hat on.

Finally, there's the **Blue Hat**. With this hat on, teams think about controlling the process, about organizing discussion, planning, and execution to achieve the best possible result. This is the process hat. This is where you ask a key question: Have we thought intelligently, hard, and long enough under all the other five hats? Blue Hat thinking promotes a process of synthesizing the creative ideas into action, managing (or accepting inevitable) risks, and moving the team forward into action. Effective teams enjoy the process of thinking laterally about the other five hats as much as the implementation hat. They see the ultimate solution as a process that integrates lateral and vertical thinking. Because all effective thinking is really logical thinking, lateral thinking is just a part of logical thinking. Blue Hat thinking leverages the inherent logic in the other five hats and brings about innovation.

Lateral thinking by teams needs to be practiced, and teams need to police the process, because many people simply cannot prevent themselves from reverting to Black Hat thinking about why something cannot work. The hat imagery helps structure the thinking (or actual, physical hats can be used, which teams can buy and have on hand in meeting rooms). However, the hats only reinforce the team's effort to synchronize, to share thinking, to be creative. Emotionally intelligent teams make a process paradigm shift, one that avoids the conflict aspects of considering new and fresh ideas, and promotes synergies instead. This synergy is potentiated by lateral thinking as a team.

The paradigm shift that highly effective teams make, really, is one of avoiding the restrictive aspects of competitive thinking, characterized by power struggles, ultimate winners, and disgruntled losers. Working as a team involves channeling the power of the team's thinking, rather than selecting between positions of power within the team. Lateral thinking reinforces awareness—both emotional awareness and awareness about potential alternatives. What the team is aware of, it can control. Conversely, things about which the team is unaware control the team—or at least impede the full thinking power of the group. Lateral thinking enhances the effectiveness of a team by increasing its awareness, and by offering it more choices, more ideas, and more from which to select.

Summary

Effective teams avoid the conflict method of considering new ideas, and find ways to get members' thinking aligned about an issue. This alignment of thinking patterns is called lateral thinking. Team leaders and team members should establish a norm that promotes the promulgation of provocative ideas, and teams should use lateral thinking to optimize the process of thinking through an issue creatively.

The "six hat" method is an excellent way for a team to introduce lateral thinking, and thereby leverage its thinking capabilities. The method requires members to work together—laterally—forsaking competition between ideas. Ultimately, a process hat helps the group move forward creatively.

The six hats reflect:

White Hat thinking—getting all available information out to the team for consideration.

Red Hat thinking—eliciting members' emotion reaction to an issue or decision.

Black Hat thinking—considering the downside of an issue or idea, what is wrong with it.

Yellow Hat thinking—focusing on why an idea is a good one, what the benefits are, what is positive about it.

Green Hat thinking—reinforcing the notion that any process is a green field opportunity to innovate. In Green Hat thinking, new provocative ideas are encouraged without judgment.

Blue Hat thinking—working through the process, to assess how the team is working. Team self-evaluations can be conducted with Blue Hat thinking. This hat helps people synthesize all the thinking that has been done.

Lateral thinking requires emotional intelligence, and with practice, can become an invaluable tool for promoting team creativity.

CHAPTER 10

Habit #6:
Entrusting Team Members
With Appropriate Roles

It's only just a matter of trust. —Billy Joel

The roles to be performed by different team members must be determined and documented. Typically, this occurs once the team's scope of work is clarified and prospective team members are identified. As the project work gets underway, members will start performing the work they were designated to perform. Well-documented role designations drive not only functional task assignments, but also team coordination processes. When all team members understand their role and the respective roles of their fellow team members, clarity is achieved about how the team's workload is distributed and who has responsibility to complete which project assignment.

Further, role designations that are well-matched to team members' respective competencies help to ensure that the project is performed skillfully. When this match is made correctly and team members do what they do best, teams develop both confidence in themselves and higher levels of mutual trust. In effective teams, members feel secure in their roles, in other team members' capabilities, and in the trust others have in them to perform in the role to which they have been assigned. Indeed, these three aspects of team performance—role designations, competence, and trust—converge, and are highly interconnected.

Figure 10: Role Designation

This sixth habit of highly effective teams, entrusting team members with appropriate roles, is a capstone attribute of highly effective teams. It builds off the other five habits we have described, and expands on the all-important element of trust that powers resonant teams. Our belief is that trust within a team cannot be dictated—it is established and grows as a result of experience, as members work together. It is established and grows as members manifest emotionally competent team behaviors and shared norms. Therefore, this habit, related to the emotional phenomenon of trust, belongs at the top of our model's structural pyramid, representing a confluence of skills, attitudes, and experiences that contribute to team trust.

Developing trust

Let's examine this emotional phenomenon called "trust" in greater depth. To understand trust is to understand how a team works well together without the need for overt, over-the-shoulder supervision of other members' work. To understand trust is to understand how a team can delegate task roles within an integrated project plan and feel comfortable that the plan will be maintained, that the service or product will be delivered with high quality and on time. There is a natural progression to trust-building in relationships, and this is certainly true of team relationships. The progression may begin with the simple awareness by team members that a team formed for a common purpose needs to trust each other, accepting the notion that the team will never get to where it wishes to go without it—indeed, accepting that if no trust exists, every team members might just as well be going it alone.

The need for trust arises from the interdependence that exists among the team members. Members depend on other people to help them obtain the outcomes that they—and the team as a group—value highly. As Roy Lewicki and Edward Tomlinson put it in their essay "Trust and Trust Building":

> As our interests with others are intertwined, we also must recognize that there is an element of risk involved insofar as we often encounter situations in which we cannot compel the cooperation we seek.

Indeed, trust involves making certain risk assessments. There are all kinds of project risks, but one of them is risk that the job may not get done right by the team member. Members cope with the discomfort of the awareness of this risk by trusting each other.

The following case example integrates several of these points about role designation, role performance, trust, and team members' willingness to assume the risk of trusting others.

Case Example

Beverly works for a managed care health insurance company in the claims department. The company's biggest account is a large telecommunications giant based in Arlington, Va. The account is managed by an account team. This team is led by the claims manager, and its members include five claims specialists, two claims supervisors, and an account representative, Sheila, who is responsible for maintaining a solid client relationship with the telecommunication company's benefits staff. Beverly is assigned a specific role on the team: processing benefit eligibility. Every Monday, she is to contact the client's benefits department and request information about any benefit eligibility changes, such as new hires, terminations, or retirements. Beverly's role is to take this information and ensure that her company's database is updated, and that the proper forms or other paperwork are exchanged with beneficiaries.

Upon arriving at work one Monday morning, she initiates her usual contact with the client's benefits department and learns that the latest eligibility data was already sent to her company, late on the previous

Friday, to Sheila, the client's account representative. Beverly then calls Sheila, who tells her, "Yes, Beverly, I saved you some work today!" Sheila tells Beverly she had asked for this information because her boss asked her to do a quality check on the data and assess how well the company performs in processing new information and following up with beneficiaries. The account representative said she retained a copy of the data received from the client and then forwarded the data on to the IT people for processing. Beverly hung up the phone, hurt and angry.

Part of the problem highlighted by this case example is a lack of communication within the team. Yet, role performance and trust are involved as well. Sheila's behavior ran counter to an implicit team norm, to allow people to perform their role on the team. Sheila's behavior essentially usurped Beverly's role, and implicitly diminished the value that Beverly brought week in and week out by owning the responsibility to reach out to the client at a set time, collect the data, and ensure that follow-up occurs. Additionally, there was an implicit lack of trust in Beverly that manifested itself in Sheila's action; the boss wanted to find out how well the team performed, so Sheila stepped on the toes of a team member to please her boss, intervening in the process to assure herself that the correct information was processed. Sheila behaved as if the only and most expeditious way to please her boss would be to take charge and get the information herself, and then tell the person typically in charge of doing so that she had done it this time. Although Sheila's need to do a quality check is not a problem in and of itself, she could have performed this function in a team context, allowing Beverly to perform her assigned role on the team.

Personality theorists have examined whether some people are more likely to trust than others. Certainly, when we have models from our life of reliable behavior, it is easier for us to trust others. Conversely, when those closest to us betray our trust, we are less likely to trust others in a similar situation. Three variables are seen by research psychologists as key in the process of establishing trusting feelings. They confirm much of what we have described, both in this chapter and throughout our 6 Habits of Highly Effective Teams model. The three variables that factor into the establishment of trusting feelings include:

▸ Evaluations of competence/ability

▸ Integrity

▸ Benevolence

The more we observe these characteristics in another person, the more likely we will be to trust in that person.

Competence/Ability refers to an assessment of anther person's knowledge and skills. This dimension recognizes that trust requires some sense that the other is able to perform in a manner that meets our expectations.

Integrity is the degree to which the trustee adheres to principles that are acceptable to the trustor. This dimension leads to trust based on consistency of past actions, credibility of communication, commitment to standards of fairness, and the alignment of the other's words and deeds (credibility). All of these factors were integral to demonstrating respect for others, described earlier in Habit #3.

Benevolence is an assessment that the trusted individual is concerned about our welfare and wishes to advance our interests—or at least not impede them. Our sense that another person feels benevolence is greatly impacted by how much empathy he or she conveys. When a team member listens, shows respect, and seeks first to understand, other members of the team will deem this as benevolent—and as such, trustworthy—behavior.

Levels of trust development

Early theories of trust described it as a unidimensional phenomenon that simply increased or decreased in magnitude and strength within a relationship. However, more recent approaches suggest that trust builds along a continuum of hierarchical and sequential stages, such that as trust grows to higher levels, it becomes stronger and more resilient and changes in character. At early stages of a relationship, trust is at a *calculus-based* level. In other words, an individual will carefully calculate how the other party is likely to behave in a given situation depending on the rewards for being trustworthy and the deterrents against untrustworthy behavior. It is a behaviorally oriented, risk and reward-based approach to trusting others. Trust will only be extended to others to the extent that a kind of cost-benefit calculation indicates that the continued trust will yield a net positive benefit. Over time, calculus-based trust can be built as individuals perceive that others wish to uphold their reputation, by behaving consistently, meeting agreed-to deadlines, and fulfilling promises. Calculus-based trust is largely a cognitively driven trust phenomenon, grounded in judgments of the trustees' predictability and reliability.

However, as different parties come to a deeper understanding of each other through repeated interactions, they become aware of shared values and goals. This allows trust to grow to a higher and qualitatively different level. When trust evolves to the highest level, it is said to function as *identity-based* trust.

At this stage trust has been built to the point that the parties have internalized each other's desires and intentions. They understand what the other party really cares about so completely that each party is able to act as an agent for the other. According to Lewicki and Tomlinson, trust at this advanced stage is also enhanced by a strong emotional bond between the parties, based on a sense of shared goals and values. So, in contrast to calculus-based trust, identity-based trust is a more emotionally driven phenomenon, grounded in perceptions of interpersonal care and concern, and mutual need satisfaction.

In the context of discussing the trust that develops within teams, the member who is able to develop deeper, more experience-based trust connects not just to the other role-performing team members, but also to the team itself. Members trust each other, and trust the team. Assignment of a role on a team and regular, competent performance in that role is part of the history of mutual need satisfaction that drives identity-based trust. Team members understand that one team member cannot do it all, and that they need to depend on others to satisfy their shared need to perform competently. But this ability to surrender control and allow oneself to depend on others is not an automatic, given process. It is built around identity-based trust. It occurs when members share values and methods, and demonstrate competence, integrity, and benevolence.

Disseminating team roles

Team role assignments should be documented on a general team contact list published for and distributed to the team. In addition to names, phone numbers, and e-mail addresses, there should be a column designating the role each respective team member performs. In project plans, task assignments should correlate with this contact/role assignment list.

Team correspondence and interactions need to reinforce role boundaries. As we reviewed in our Case Example in this chapter, nothing discourages a teammate faster than having his or her role usurped. Behaviors that violate role boundaries run counter to healthy team norms, and should be confronted. When a team member's role does change, the change needs to be thoroughly explained by the project team leader, and disseminated throughout the entire team. If the change is warranted due to poor project performance, then the need for this should be rather obvious to the team. It is the more sudden and abrupt role changes that upset a team's equilibrium, and should be avoided if possible. Certainly, unilateral changes by a team leader, without rationale or explanation, will diminish or eradicate team trust rather quickly.

Flexing to team roles and members' people style

Competent role performance can be connected to the relevant member's people style, according to Robert and Dorothy Bolton. Certain team roles just *fit* a team member better than another. When the fit is quite right, team competence and mutual trust often is heightened. When the fit is wrong, the role assignment may be a mistake, and team competence and trust may suffer. For example, **Amiables** are great in highly supportive, service-oriented team roles, where this service orientation adds value to the team's responsiveness to client requirements. **Drivers** may be better than **Amiables** as task leads or in other roles requiring someone to own responsible for meeting tight deadlines. **Expressives** may be best at leading and facilitating a public presentation in front of a client, because they keep everyone "loose" and relaxed, and they connect well with the audience. Clearly, **Analyticals** are well-suited for budget discussions and procedure-heavy tasks.

The point is that matching members to the role for which they are most likely to succeed and gain others' trust can be a strategic decision that takes into account people styles as well as prior experience. Just because a member has performed a role in a previous team does not mean that he or she is the best to perform the same role in a different team. Experience is a factor, but so too is his or her interpersonal style and personality. Teams trust each other more when the fit between roles and people styles is good, and this trust can diminish when there is no match in what a member is asked to do and the personality the member brings to the task.

Summary

Teams need to assign members to appropriate roles, and allow them to perform in this role. Role boundaries are sensitive—violations of role boundaries are likely to diminish team morale and trust considerably. Team trust is contingent on appropriate role designations, competent performance in these roles, team integrity, and the benevolence that team members demonstrate to others on the project. When teams move from trusting each other based on risk-reward ratios, and move toward an identity-based trust formed through acknowledgement of shared beliefs and values, the emotional atmosphere in the team is conducive to performing all the other five habits in our model. Teams that trust each other form a cohesive whole, which is the foundation of team effectiveness.

Afterword

The application of these six habits that promote team effectiveness is up to you. You now know what these habits are, and you have the tools and specific suggestions for promoting these habits within your teams. We promised that our model would be practical, and one that can be applied to yield rather rapid results. We assured you that incorporating these habits would not overwhelm you, either due to their difficulty or due to the enormity of the challenge in applying them. The model is built upon several simple and straightforward understandings:

▶ **You need to understand what emotional intelligence is,** and build both your own and your team's EI. Think of the concept of building EI as one you wish to apply to yourself, to the team, and to the teams customers.

▶ **Always seek feedback,** which the team should digest and use to form an accurate assessment of what it does well and what it could improve.

▶ **Document your team's beliefs and norms, then reinforce what has been developed about these team identity factors every day.** Expand your team's emotional literacy and comfort in emotional situations.

▶ **Build and apply superior listening skills.** Communication in teams is all about listening to each other.

▶ **Seek first to understand.** It's not about you, it's about "us."

▶ **Respect each other, and your respective roles on the team.** This will lead to the development of team trust.

▶ **Avoid competitive thinking; seek ways to think together.** Embrace the most creative and provocative thoughts as gifts from each other.

▶ **Frame issues around the team**—use "we" and "the team" rather than "I."

▶ **Depersonalize conflict.** Frame the conflict around ideas and challenges, not people on the team.

Is there more to our model than these nine themes? Sure. But the engrained behaviors that demonstrate our six habits revolve around them. According to both research and our empirical observation, the objective of team skill-building is the development of team cohesion—thinking and processes that elicit a feeling of sharing and caring. Team cohesion feels great! It is an emotional high. When shared values and superior performance come together in a group environment, well, it just doesn't get any better than that! We encourage you to go for it.

Appendix A

Please turn the page for our
Team Self-Evaluation Survey.

Instructions: Circle the frequency rating that applies best to your team.

Team characteristic: Our team...	Habit #(s)*	4 Always	3 Most often	2 Sometimes	1 Not very often or never	0 No opinion
Demonstrates competence in performing its project(s).	1, 6	4	3	2	1	●
Demonstrates honesty—within the group and with outside clients and stakeholders.	1, 3	4	3	2	1	●
Makes successful efforts to understand the needs of external clients and stakeholders.	1, 3	4	3	2	1	●
Is easy to work with, from the clients'/stakeholders' viewpoint.	1	4	3	2	1	●
Remains fully accessible, to each other and to clients/stakeholders.	1	4	3	2	1	●

Statement						
Follows up routinely and comprehensively to requests or action items generated internally and externally.	1	4	3	2	1	•
Shares information openly and comprehensively.	1	4	3	2	1	•
Is attentive to promoting working relationships among individual team members.	1, 3, 4, 6	4	3	2	1	•
Is skilled in developing working relationships among individual team members.	1, 3, 4, 6	4	3	2	1	•
Is attentive to working relationships between members and the team itself.	1	4	3	2	1	•
Is skilled in developing working relationships between members and the team itself.	1	4	3	2	1	•
Is attentive to working relationships between the team and external clients/stakeholders.	1	4	3	2	1	•
Is aware of its emotional temperature.	1, 2	4	3	2	1	•

	Habit #(s)*	Always	Most often	Sometimes	Not very often or never	No opinion
Is aware of its strengths and weaknesses.	2	4	3	2	1	●
Has documented its mission.	2	4	3	2	1	●
Adheres to its mission.	2	4	3	2	1	●
Recognizes what excellent performance looks like.	2	4	3	2	1	●
Embraces measurement and analysis of its performance against quality standards.	2	4	3	2	1	●
Allots time periodically for group reflection on team norms, behaviors, and effectiveness.	1, 2	4	3	2	1	●
Has a distinct identity.	2	4	3	2	1	●
Listens actively** in team forums of all kinds.	3	4	3	2	1	●
Uncovers content or emotions in the group that have been left unspoken.	3	4	3	2	1	●

			4	3	2	1	•
Seeks first to understand.	3		4	3	2	1	•
Is courteous in all internal and external interactions.	3		4	3	2	1	•
Embraces diversity within the team.	3		4	3	2	1	•
Has a set of established norms, both implicit and explicit, that regulate group behavior.	1, 2, 4		4	3	2	1	•
Adheres to these implicit and explicit norms.	4		4	3	2	1	•
Demonstrates an ability to think creatively and innovatively when the project requires creativity and innovation.	5		4	3		1	•
Is able to think together about all aspects of an issue, rather than in an oppositional way (deciding between relative strengths of opposing ideas).	5		4	3	2	1	•

	Habit #(s)*	Always	Most often	Sometimes	Not very often or never	No opinion
Has members in assigned roles for which they are competent.	6	4	3	2	1	●
Has members in assigned roles matched well to their basic personality style.	6	4	3	2	1	●
Understands each member's role on the team.	6	4	3	2	1	●
Accepts each member's role on the team.	6	4	3	2	1	●
Trusts that other members will perform competently.	6	4	3	2	1	●
Is highly effective.	1–6	4	3	2	1	●

Subtotals: _____
Sum of Subtotals: _____

Scoring the Self-Evaluation: Your average score is the sum of your subtotals, divided by the number you obtain when you subtract your amount of "no opinion" responses from 35.

Average = _____

▲ **3.5 – 4.0 — Superior team cohesion**

▲ **3.0 – 3.5 — Good team cohesion**

▲ **2.5 – 3.0 — Fair team cohesion**

▲ **< 2.5 — Lacks consistent team cohesion**

* This designation of a match between a team characteristic and one or more of the six habits is in no way to be construed as exclusive to the noted habit number; indeed, in many cases the characteristic touches all the habits, at least indirectly. However, we note the closest match based on our descriptions of the relevant issues and team behaviors for each of the respective habits.

** Listening actively is defined in Habit #3, and includes behaviors such as: rephrasing content, reflecting the feeling, probing with open-ended questions, supporting, and providing feedback.

Appendix B

Exercise in Emotional Literacy

This list of adjectives was developed to help members of teams find the most appropriate description of perceived feelings. No attempt has been made to order these words in terms of their degree of intensity.

Also note that by simply preceding these adjectives with other, quantitative adjectives, you can control the intensity of your communication.

For example:

▶ You feel *somewhat* angry when a teammate criticizes your work.

▶ You feel *quite* angry when a teammate criticizes your work.

▶ You feel *very* angry when a teammate criticizes your work.

▶ You feel *extremely* angry when a teammate criticizes your work.

Exercise: Try to differentiate the meanings of each these words, by applying them to personal experience within teams, within activities at work in general, or if necessary, in your personal life.

"The last time I felt [**insert emotional vocabulary word here**] when working in a team [*you may substitute "working in an organization" or if necessary, "in my personal life"*], I was [**insert your memory of the team/work/personal circumstances when you felt the vocabulary word**]."

Pleasant affective states

Love, affection, concern

admired	adorable	affectionate	agreeable
altruistic	amiable	benevolent	benign
big-hearted	brotherly	caring	charitable
Christian	comforting	congenial	conscientious
considerate	cooperative	cordial	courteous
dedicated	easygoing	empathetic	fair

faithful	forgiving	friendly	generous
genuine	giving	good	good-natured
good-humored	helpful	honest	honorable
hospitable	humane	interested	just
kind	kindly	kind-hearted	lenient
lovable	loving	mellow	mild
moral	neighborly	nice	obliging
open	optimistic	patient	peaceful
pleasant	reasonable	receptive	reliable
respectful	responsible	sensitive	sympathetic
sweet	tender	thoughtful	tolerant
trustworthy	understanding	unselfish	warm
warm-hearted	well-meaning	wise	

Elation, joy

amused	at ease	blissful	brilliant
calm	cheerful	comical	contented
delighted	ecstatic	elated	elevated
enchanted	enthusiastic	exalted	excellent
excited	fantastic	fine	gay
glad	glorious	good	grand
gratified	great	happy	humorous
inspired	in high spirits	jovial	joyful
jubilant	magnificent	majestic	overjoyed
pleased	pleasant	proud	satisfied
serene	splendid	superb	terrific
thrilled	tremendous	triumphant	turned on
vivacious	witty	wonderful	

Potency

able	adequate	assured	authoritative
bold	brave	capable	competent
confident	courageous	determined	durable
dynamic	effective	energetic	fearless
firm	forceful	gallant	hardy
healthy	heroic	important	influential
intense	lion-hearted	manly	mighty
powerful	robust	secure	self-confident
self-reliant	skillful	spirited	stable
stouthearted	strong	sure	tough
virile	well-equipped	well put together	

Unpleasant affective states

Depression

abandoned	alien	alienated	alone
annihilated	awful	battered	below par
blue	burned	cast off	cheapened
crushed	debased	defeated	degraded
dejected	demolished	depressed	desolate
despairing	despised	despondent	destroyed
discarded	discouraged	disfavored	dismal
done for	downcast	down-hearted	downtrodden
dreadful	estranged	excluded	forlorn
forsaken	gloomy	glum	grim
hated	hopeless	horrible	humiliated

hurt	in the dumps	jilted	kaput
left out	loathed	lonely	lonesome
lousy	low	miserable	mishandled
mistreated	moody	mournful	obsolete
ostracized	out of sorts	overlooked	pathetic
pitiful	rebuked	regretful	rejected
reprimanded	rotten	ruined	run down
sad	stranded	tearful	terrible
unhappy	unloved	valueless	washed up
whipped	worthless	wrecked	

Distress

afflicted	anguished	at the feet of	at the mercy of
awkward	baffled	bewildered	blameworthy
clumsy	confused	constrained	disgusted
disliked	displeased	dissatisfied	distrustful
disturbed	doubtful	foolish	futile
grieved	helpless	hindered	impaired
impatient	imprisoned	lost	nauseated
offended	pained	perplexed	puzzled
ridiculous	sickened	silly	skeptical
speechless	strained	suspicious	swamped
plaything of	puppet of	tormented	ungainly
unlucky	unpopular	unsatisfied	unsure

Fear, anxiety

afraid	agitated	alarmed	anxious
apprehensive	bashful	desperate	dreading

embarrassed	fearful	fidgety	frightened
hesitant	horrified	ill at ease	insecure
intimidated	jealous	jittery	jumpy
nervous	on edge	overwhelmed	panicky
restless	scared	shaky	shy
strained	tense	terrified	terror-stricken
timid	uncomfortable	uneasy	worried

Belittling, criticism, scorn

abused	belittled	branded	carped at
caviled at	censured	criticized	defamed
deflated	deprecated	depreciated	derided
diminished	discredited	disdained	disgraced
disparaged	humiliated	ignored	jeered
lampooned	laughed at	libeled	made light of
maligned	minimized	mocked	neglected
overlooked	poked fun at	pooh-poohed	pulled to pieces
put down	ridiculed	roasted	scoffed at
scorned	shamed	slandered	slighted
underestimated	underrated		

Impotency, inadequacy

anemic	broken	broken down	chicken-hearted
cowardly	crippled	debilitated	defective
deficient	demoralized	disabled	exhausted
exposed	feeble	flimsy	fragile
frail	harmless	helpless	impotent
inadequate	incapable	incompetent	indefensible

ineffective	inefficient	inept	inferior
infirm	insecure	insufficient	lame
maimed	meek	nerveless	paralyzed
powerless	puny	shaken	shaky
sickly	small	strengthless	trivial
unable	uncertain	unfit	unimportant
unqualified	unsound	unsubstantiated	useless
vulnerable	weak	weak-hearted	

Anger, hostility, cruelty

angry	aggravated	aggressive	annoyed
antagonistic	arrogant	austere	bad-tempered
belligerent	bigoted	biting	bloodthirsty
blunt	bullying	callous	cold-blooded
combative	cantankerous	contrary	cool
corrosive	cranky	critical	cross
cruel	deadly	dictatorial	disagreeable
discontented	dogmatic	enraged	envious
exasperated	fierce	furious	gruesome
hard	hard-hearted	harsh	hateful
heartless	hellish	hideous	hostile
hypocritical	ill-tempered	impatient	inconsiderate
inhuman	insensitive	intolerable	intolerant
irritated	mad	malicious	mean
murderous	nasty	obstinate	opposed
oppressive	outraged	perturbed	poisonous
prejudiced	pushy	rebellious	reckless

resentful	revengeful	rough	rude
ruthless	sadistic	savage	severe
spiteful	stern	stormy	unfeeling
unfriendly	unmerciful	unruly	vicious
vindictive	violent	wrathful	

Bibliography

Arrow, H., J.E. McGrath, and J.L. Berdahl. *Small Groups as Complex Systems: Formation, Coordination, Development, and Adaptation*. Newbury Park, Calif.: Sage, 2000.

Bolton, Robert H., and Dorothy G. Bolton. *People Styles at Work*. New York: Amacom, 1996.

Campbell, John, J. David Flynn, James Hay. "The Group Development Process Seen Through the Lens of Complexity Theory 1." *www.fss.uu.nl/ms/cvd/isj/pdflyn.pdf.*

Capon, Noel. *Key Account Management and Planning.* New York: Simon and Schuster, 2001.

Cohen, Susan G., and Diane E. Bailey. "What Makes Teams Work: Group Effectiveness Research from the Shop Floor to the Executive Suite." *Journal of Management* 23, no. 3 (1997): 239–90.

Covey, Steven R. *7 Habits of Highly Effective People.* New York: Simon & Schuster, 1989.

de Bono, Edward. *Six Thinking Hats.* New York: Little Brown, 1999.

———. *Lateral Thinking.* New York: Harper & Row, 1990.

Druskatt, V.U., and S.B. Wolff. "Building the Emotional Intelligence of Groups." *Harvard Business Review* 79, no. 3 (2001): 80.

Forsyth, D.R. "The Social Psychology of Groups and Group Psychotherapy: One View of the Next Century." *Group* 24:147–55.

Globecon Group, "The Role of Relationship Management." *www.globecon.com/solutions/ relationship_management.html.*

Goleman, Daniel. *Working With Emotional Intelligence.* New York: Bantam Books, 1998.

Heuerman, Tom, Ph.D. "Mission, Teams and Loyalty." *Selfhelp Magazine. www.selfhelpmagazine.com/articles/ wf/mission-teams-loyalty.html.*

Kang, Hye-Ryun, Hee-Dong Yang, and Chris Rowley. "Factors in Team Effectiveness: Cognitive and Demographic Similarities of Software Development Team Members." *Human Relations* 59, no.12 (2006): 1681–1710.

Katzenbach, Jon R., and Douglas K. Smith. *The Wisdom of Teams.* New York: HarperCollins, 2003.

Kohn, Stephen E., and Vincent D. O'Connell. *6 Habits of Highly Effective Bosses.* Franklin Lakes, N.J.: Career Press, 2005.

Leader to Leader, "Leading Resonant Teams: An Interview with Daniel Goleman."*media.wiley.com/assets/66/63/ jrnls_LTL_JB_goleman25.pdf.*

Lewicki, Roy J., and Edward C. Tomlinson. "Trust and Trust Building." Beyond Intractability (2003): *www.beyondintractability.org/essay/trust_building.*

Lewin, Kurt. *Resolving social conflicts; selected papers on group dynamics.* New York: Harper & Row, 1948.

Pickering, Marisue. "Communication." *Explorations: A Journal of Research of the University of Maine* 3, no. 1 (1986): 16–19.

Roethlisberger, F.J., and W.J. Dickson. *Management and the Worker.* Cambridge, Mass.: Harvard University Press, 1939.

Stubbs, Elizabeth Christine. "Emotional Intelligence Competencies in the Team and Team Leader: A Multi-Level Examination of the Impact of Emotional Intelligence on Group Performance." Ph.D. diss., Case Western University, 2005.

Sherman, Sallie, Joseph Sperry, and Samuel Reese. *The Seven Keys to Managing Strategic Accounts.* New York: McGraw-Hill, 2003.

Tuckerman, B.W., and M.A.C. Jensen. "Stages of Small Group Development Revisited." *Group and Organizational Studies* 2 (1977): 419–27.

Wardwell, Walter I. "Critique of a Recent Professional 'Put-Down' of the Hawthorne Research." *American Sociological Review* 44, no. 5 (1979): 858–61. doi: 10.2307/2094533.

For a graphic and content presentation of the Drexler/Sibbet Team Performance Model, see *www.northeasternconsulting.com/ newsletter/Drexler_Sibbet_Model.pdf.*

INDEX

About the Authors

Mr. Stephen Kohn is president of Work & People Solutions, a human resources management, leadership development, and executive coaching firm based in White Plains, New York. He is one of the most senior and experienced executive coaches in the world, having been a senior vice president for more than a decade at one of the pioneering executive coaching firms,

Paul Sherman and Associates. Throughout his career, Mr. Kohn has led account management teams for professional services firms, primarily focused on business development and client relationship management. He is the coauthor of *6 Habits of Highly Effective Bosses*, and he has appeared as a guest commentator on topics relating to organizational leadership for numerous media, including WCBS radio in New York and Newsday in Long Island, N.Y. He graduated from Cornell University and completed his graduate studies at Adelphi University. He has professional licensure in New York and New Jersey to provide mental health services. Mr. Kohn is also an adjunct professor of management at Long Island University, teaching MBA courses dedicated to work, people, and productivity.

Mr. Vincent O'Connell is senior partner of Work & People Solutions. He leads the firm's assessment and training services, which provide 360-degree multi-rater feedback surveys and a wide range of team-building and people management learning programs to organizations worldwide. He also manages teams developing various business proposals, consulting for the business development function of information technology firms that contract with the federal government. Earlier in his career, Mr. O'Connell served in executive positions in marketing at various hospitals, and he was a consultant for the Hay Group. A graduate of Brown University, Mr. O'Connell did his graduate work in human resources management at Cornell University. He has authored numerous articles for professional journals, and coauthored *6 Habits of Highly Effective Bosses* with Mr. Kohn. He also writes fiction, and he is currently completing work on his second novel.

Other titles available from Career Press

6 Habits of Highly Effective Bosses
by Stephen E. Kohn and Vincent D. O'Connell

The Sexual Harrassment Handbook
by Linda Gordon Howard

Don't Take the Last Donut
by Judith Bowman

Quick & Painless Business Writing
by Susan F. Benjamin